A Minor Indiscretion:
Captured In Morocco

A Minor Indiscretion

Graham Hutt

First published 2004 by Authentic Media
9 Holdom Avenue, Bletchley, Milton Keynes, Bucks,
MK1 1QR, UK
and PO Box 1047, Waynesboro, GA 30830-2047, USA

British Library Cataloguing in Publication Data

A catalogue record for this book is available from the
British Library

1-85078-578-3

Cover design by Peter Barnsley
Print Management by Adare Carwin
Printed and bound by AIT Nørhaven A/S, Denmark

Contents

Prologue

This is an unfinished story. If I had been able to pursue justice and draw a line under the events surrounding my arrest and imprisonment, albeit for only a brief period of time, it would never have been written. I have read accounts of great suffering, and in comparison, this saga was a minor scrape with an unjust judge and officials, who themselves will be judged one day.

A deep and life-changing impression remains with me to this day. It has enabled me to realize just how much others suffer as a consequence of the ignorance or greed of those in authority. Control is so easily exercised by denying education to the masses; even the simple right to read the books they choose. Authorities well understand the power of the printed word, and the danger posed by an educated people.

This book is written to highlight the plight of others, who find themselves in the same position as myself, but do not have the same ability to shout 'Foul!' I feel no anger. Indeed, I have a continuing deep love and appreciation for the Arab people, and for the many devout Muslims I have known over the past thirty years.

The adoption of our Arab daughter Ghada furthers the commitment of my whole family to their culture. It is one that I have studied and worked within for many years. During that time, I learned the importance of 'saving face' and how a perceived cause of humiliation can bring consequences.

It is possible that the following adventure was the result of a single inadvertent event necessitating revenge. The initiation and defence of corrupt practices became an inevitable consequence, even extending to an attempt to override the orders of the King. Often, the secular authorities in the Islamic world have been the ones to cause pain and anxiety to their people. It is those same people who do not understand or care about the teachings or intentions of their own religious masters and founder.

This story begins in 1998, when a French couple, two Canadians (of Finnish origin) and myself were arrested. One of them was found to be in possession of a small black bag containing something the police and a judge were to deem 'illegal in Morocco' – Bibles. The penalties totalled nearly half a million Dollars, plus imprisonment. A pronouncement that contributed to his death.

The names of some of those involved have been changed in the recounting of this drama.

1. Unwelcome Visitors

Sunday 31st May 1998

It was nine o'clock exactly, on a quiet Sunday morning. The rattle of diesel engines sounded outside the yacht. My eyes followed the noise through the window, which was at the level of the quay, due to the low tide. Several pairs of black, laced boots were visible. These men were here to arrest us.

A voice shouted: 'Captain, Captain.' For once, I wished I were not the captain. After thirty years of sailing experience I had grown to know my abilities and to feel comfortable in making decisions, even in the most extreme and dangerous of circumstances at sea. Suddenly I was no longer in control and did not even know where we would be taken or for how long. As I walked up the companionway ladder and acknowledged their presence, I told them to wait, while I returned below for my pullover. Without looking in their direction, I listened for any reaction as I descended. There was none.

Despite the fact that we did not get to bed before three o'clock that morning, we had been up for over two hours. The Canadians, Veikko and Matti clambered up and stepped reluctantly onto the dockside.

As I locked up the yacht, my mind was preoccupied as I thought of anything I might have forgotten to do. Had I turned off the batteries and the water pump? Did I hide the valuable electronics and hand-bearing compass? I glanced towards the bow-lines to check that the ropes were secure with the correct tension on the bollards. Occasional severe storms hit this area, and my yacht was a heavy displacement vessel designed for sailing open oceans, rather than being incarcerated and unattended in the confines of a harbour. We could be away for a day, months or a year.

Once ashore, one of the policemen asked, 'Do you have any books on board?'

I held my hand out, palm uppermost towards the yacht, and told him 'Come, see for yourself!'

He smiled and walked to the rear of a white, rusty Citroën van. I could read *Surte:* 'Police' written in Arabic, along the side. Another Citroën was behind, and standing beside it with a policeman, were my French friends Jacques and his wife Françoise, who lived in the marina. I wondered if we would all be separated or handcuffed, but we were not.

The police, who were the same as those involved in the car chase and wild activity of the night before, now milled around almost aimlessly. A plume of smoke settled above their heads on this windless day, as they drew heavily on their Camel cigarettes. They seemed friendly enough, quite different from the previous night.

The chief of police in the marina, who I now knew to be Mohammed, spoke good English. He came up to me and putting his hand on my shoulders, said, ominously, 'Be brave Graham, be strong.' His comment struck a note of fear, deep in the pit of my stomach. As the officers indicated that we should climb into the back of one of the vans, it seemed as if we were going on a Sunday outing, at least until that last remark from Mohammed. Recalling the previous night, I was unsure whether he was trying to give comfort or was merely being sarcastic.

However helpful or prophetic it was supposed to sound, I had thought back to that moment, a few short hours before, when he had roared around the marina in the dead of night in his battered black Ford Capri. Tyres had squealed as he weaved between startled pedestrians, who fled to the pavement. Although so recent, it seemed like a film I had seen in the distant past.

Our circumstances had changed fast and un-expectedly. We had arrived in this marina the evening before and uneventfully encountered these same police-men, most of whom I had recognized from many previous visits. Marina Smir had become the base for my work on a book,[1] which was almost complete: a sailing guide and pilot covering the entire coast of North Africa, from the Tunisian border with Libya, to the Atlantic Moroccan frontier with Mauritania. Morocco was the last country to be re-checked and this marina was closest to my home in Spain.

One of the final tasks before publication was to obtain rare aerial photographs of the Atlantic ports. I had seen these being prepared for an exhibition in Portugal while visiting the Ministry of Ports and Fisheries several weeks earlier. An official had promised that at the end of the exhibition, he would give them to me. I had an appoint-ment to meet with the Minister of Tourism the following Monday.

The conditions had been perfect as we sailed across the Straits of Gibraltar. A gentle easterly wind with negli-

---

[1] Graham Hutt, *North Africa,* (St Ives: Imray, Laurie, Norie and Wilson Ltd, 2000)

gible swell had prevailed. The journey took less than eight hours from the port of Sotogrande in Spain, and it was unnecessary to start the engine, until nearing the port. We had made a diversion around the long tuna nets that were placed outside the marina. The nets stretched north for three miles or more towards the towns of Fnidiq and Sebta, and were a great navigational hazard to the unsuspecting yachtsman. Frequently, boats got entangled in them at night, as they were often not lit up.

Dusk had been closing in fast, and we could just make out the small boat marking the southern end of the net as we approached the marina. This corresponded exactly with the position I had entered into the navigational computer on a previous visit. Fog often descended suddenly at sunset in this area, especially when the wind was a light easterly. I was therefore always careful to check my position, even though the lights on land were clearly visible.

It had been peaceful as we dropped the sails, and motored the last mile with a decreasing wind, the sun dropping behind Jebel Zem Zem, part of the Rif Mountain range that constitutes the wonderfully scenic backdrop to this marina. As I turned the wheel hard to starboard heading into the port, I asked Matti to let down the fenders, and we were soon approaching the temporary visitors' berth next to the marina office, where customs and immigration formalities are first to be completed before a berth is allocated.

A marina helper came from the office and took our ropes. As soon as we were secured alongside, I walked up the steps and went inside to meet the officials with Matti – passports and ship registration papers in hand. Although it seemed late, the office was still open due to the two-hour time difference between Spain and Morocco.[2] Several police and customs officers were sitting around outside their offices drinking mint tea and smoking, as they always did.

Recognizing the yacht as we had sailed in the previous evening, one of these same policemen, now here to arrest us, had been the friendly voice shouting out my name. There were few visitors to the marina and I was probably one of their most frequent guests. I had replied: 'Naam,' which I knew was the Lebanese way of saying 'yes', rather than the Moroccan 'aiwa', but I was always reluctant to use my Arabic here, as the people became suspicious when I did so. A barrage of questions about where I learned it and why always followed, indicating their suspicion – questions that were not easy to answer, especially as the real reason was simple.

I loved the Arab people and their culture, and had spent a lot of time in many of their countries. This explanation was always rejected and the questions were rephrased to get a different answer. There wasn't one. The fact that one of our children, Ghada, was an adopted Arab girl, made them all the more suspicious. I began learning Arabic in Lebanon in 1981, whilst my wife Anne remained with the children – two boys and two girls – who were in school in Cyprus. My first visit to the Levant was as a volunteer to work with World Vision. Ghada, who was three years old when we adopted her in Jordan, was in an orphanage almost from the time of her birth, and was so traumatized that she never learned the Arabic language. It was many years later that she began to speak, and it was only then that we discovered she suffered the symptoms of autism.

---

[2] Morocco keeps Greenwhich Mean Time all year round.

The receptionist handed us the usual entry forms, which we completed for the passport officer and the customs authorities. The customs form was the standard one used throughout the world: the captain declares that there are no firearms, ammunition or excess quantities of tobacco or spirits. I always carried a carton or two of cigarettes to give as *baksheesh*[3] to the many helpful people I met in Morocco. Almost no spirits were on board and I never carried firearms, although many yachts did. I happily signed. Our passports were stamped and handed back. Then we were allocated a berth on the opposite side of the marina.

With the formalities completed, we returned to the yacht. A customs officer was standing on the quay with a policeman. I invited both to come aboard to give their usual inspection. The police officer seemed interested only in my shelves of books, while the customs officer looked briefly in all the cabins. He took one book from the shelf and glanced through it before returning it, without comment. They both made their way to the companionway after less than two minutes, welcoming us to Morocco, and wishing us a happy stay.

Matti behaved like an excited schoolboy as we motored the short distance, across the deserted marina to our mooring. His previous experience in Morocco had been horrendous, but he was looking forward to this trip with me to see the 'real' Morocco. I was sure he would enjoy his stay here, and was convinced I would show him the wonderful nature of the people – their true side. How could I have known what was about to unfold, or that he would never recover from the trauma of the events?

I took a last look around as I stepped up into the back of the police van. Before the doors closed, I noticed how

---

[3] An expected gift given for a service.

bleak the place looked. This marina was one of the best ever built: splendid in every respect.

The port architecture was a fine example of modern elegant Moroccan design, having been constructed by Bulgarians ten years ago as part of a trade deal in return for phosphates, one of Morocco's principal exports. Like most other well-built marinas, it had every facility a captain could want for himself and his crew, and was capable of harbouring over four hundred yachts.

Yet in one respect, this marina was different. It was completely empty. I had never seen a marina so large with usually no more than two yachts berthed. Apart from the police and customs launches at the far side it was deserted. Even on the occasions when I had been here in the height of summer, there were not more than a handful of day-visiting boats. This marina had a reputation. It was often used for the lucrative drug trade to Spain and Gibraltar. The town of Katama, famous for its high quality marijuana, was nearby.

Although I had never experienced any problems here – except for two incidents that I later recalled – this was unusual. Yachts not engaged in the drug trade almost always experienced hassle from police and customs officials. This usually took the form of demands for bottles of whisky and cartons of cigarettes. If not provided, extensive searching and general harassment followed. I was used to this, and found it better to give them what they wanted. Many Americans and Germans would not comply and were outraged by these demands. Rarely did they stay more than one night.

As we departed in the Citroën, I once again felt its sinister nature. Over the months to come, I was to discover much more about this marina.

2. The Journey to Tetouan

Sunday 31st May 11am

As we were driven out of the port, the high ramps jolted the van so hard that I banged my head against the metal side frame. At the top of the road, we turned left towards the small coastal town of M'Diq. I had wondered if we would be turning right, towards the Spanish border and the enclave of Ceuta, known to Moroccans as Sebta. At least we weren't simply going to be expelled from the country.

M'Diq appeared to have an enormous number of policemen and our driver waved to every one on the street, stopping to greet some of them with a brief hand-shake. A stream of traffic piled up behind us; angry horns sounding impatiently. We seemed to be in no hurry. As we passed through the town, we turned right towards Tetouan. Since the main police headquarters were located there, it had not taken long to guess where we were heading.

To my surprise, just as we accelerated onto the main highway, we pulled over and stopped. Two high iron gates opened and from the Arabic sign I could see that this was a police station. I had sat opposite this building on many occasions, drinking coffee or mint tea, while remaining oblivious to its identity. The gates were closed and the rear doors of the van opened. We were told to get out. The early morning chill was still in the air and birds were singing in the palm trees above our heads. A great picnic spot, I mused.

We were herded into the building, along a corridor and into a bare room. A large picture of King Hassan II hung behind a dirty, steel-framed desk. A police officer stood up and spoke in Arabic. While we shrugged and looked at each other, another officer spoke in French. Jacques replied saying a few words, looking at me, but I did not understand. I always had difficulty knowing what he was saying, but now he was very nervous and communication was impossible. Françoise did not even try to converse in English. We were signalled to sit down on a narrow wooden plank along a wall opposite the desk. Jacques, a burly man, looked as if he had been a fighter in his youth. Françoise was the opposite, very petite and frail.

The officers who had escorted us walked out into a yard leading directly off the room, and peered through the tiny grille of what appeared to be a cell. I stood up and sauntered over to see what was there. No one stopped me, so I went outside and was beckoned by one officer to look through the grille. To my horror, a man was chained to the wall, wrists fastened to an iron ring above his head. Although it was dark inside the cell, the sun shone through, and his ragged appearance and etched features were clearly visible. His head hung down with his chin supported by his chest. He did not look up in response to our presence. One officer looked at me with a terrifying grin. Hastily, I retreated to the bench, and began to think the worst. Was this to be our fate?

After an hour or more, two policemen came in and tried to converse with me. Although I had picked up Arabic in the Middle East, the Moroccan dialect was quite different. They were able to understand me, since most of the films they watched were made in the Middle East but I only partially understood them. One of the officers left and returned with a man who spoke some English. I was told that the officers wanted me to return to the yacht. My heart leapt, as I thought this meant freedom.

'What about my friends?' I asked. No, they have to stay. Was this because they had realized that I was innocent of any supposedly committed 'crime' and that I just happened to be the captain?

I asked our interpreter to explain to the police that as captain I wanted to take responsibility for the problem and wanted the others freed as well, even if this meant I had to stay. After speaking with the officer, he smiled as he said that I had misunderstood. The police wanted me to return while they searched the yacht. I would be brought back here later.

Despondent once again, I was taken to the van, still parked in the same place in the courtyard. A young boy was pouring fuel into the tank from a plastic can. Much of it spilled onto the ground. The place stank of diesel. One officer jumped in the back with me, and the other, along with a driver, sat in the front. We went out through the gates and headed back in the direction of the marina.

As we continued our journey, I thought through what they might find, but could not envisage anything that could be a problem. I had owned the yacht for over ten years, and for much of that time it had been home for me and my family. I began to wonder if it was really *baksheesh* they wanted. They knew I was more familiar with the culture than the others. Was this their way of separating me, in order to get money? This was a real possibility, the most likely, I thought. Perhaps all they wanted was a bottle of whisky or some cigarettes.

These thoughts took me back to an experience in this same port two years before, when an officer came aboard and announced that he had been ordered to search my yacht. It was midnight. After allowing him on board, he immediately demanded a bottle of whisky. I had none, so I offered him a can of beer. To my surprise he opened it, tilted his head back and drank asking for more. Unsure what to do, I protested that as a good Muslim, he should not be drinking.

He began to get quite obnoxious and asked for my wife. She emerged from the rear cabin, having heard the commotion. I explained what was happening. If he did not leave, I would call other policemen, who I knew would be close. I was reluctant to do this, as it meant leaving her alone with him, and he seemed quite unpredictable.

For another half an hour, I tried to be polite and gave him a glass of wine. But he became more verbally abusive as time went on. Finally I was so exasperated that I went to call for help.

A guardian was stationed at the end of every jetty. They understood Spanish as they were hired locally. I spoke to the first one I saw, explaining the problem and asked him to summons the police to remove their drunken colleague. Two officers came over and apologized as they came onboard. Seeing their difficulty as they carried him off made me realize just how very drunk he was.

But there was also a second, far more sinister incident. It dawned on me that there could be a connection between this and the current situation.

One night at around ten o'clock the year before when I was in this same marina, a policeman approached the yacht, calling my name. The tall, gaunt-looking man wearing a suit gently explained in perfect English that he was a police officer, and needed to come on board. After asking the reason, he replied that his chief had told him to check my books.

'What books?' I asked.

'That is what I want to see.'

I could think of no books of interest to him, but motioned for him to come aboard.

He was intelligent, quite pleasant and he smelled of cologne.

'I need to look at your books,' he repeated.

I invited him to go ahead. In the main cabin there were two long bookshelves containing over two hundred books. They included a wide range of medical and alternative therapy books; tomes on psychology and anthropology, my sailing books and nautical pilots covering the entire Mediterranean. I also had a huge collection of small tourist booklets and maps, collected from all over the world.

The policeman began by removing books from the shelf, placing them in a pile on the table and then reading the title page of each one. My sailing pilots were his first choice. He asked permission to sit down and make notes. Each book was meticulously lifted from the pile, as he copied down the author, publisher, and dates of publication details before reaching for the next book.

Several times I asked for his name, but he refused to tell me. More than an hour later, he had filled two sides of a page and had only looked at fifteen books. I wanted to go to bed and asked him to return in the morning. He just continued to write. In fact, none of my questions concerning why he was there were answered. I was so sure his visit had nothing to do with the books but could think of no logical reason.

Many thoughts went through my mind. Should I just demand that he stopped this ridiculous exercise and leave? Or, should I harass him and hope he tired of the intrusions? I just could not figure out why he wanted this information and was confused. He seemed such a gentleman. Surely, he would soon have enough information to satisfy his chief. Of one thing I was certain: he would find nothing illegal or offensive to his religion amongst my books.

He came to one of Ghada's colouring books. When he opened the cover and began to copy the details, I could contain my anger no longer and shouted: 'Stop! Are you, as a Muslim, afraid of a child's English colouring book? What do you really want?' I demanded.

He repeated softly, 'It's for my chief. I am your friend. Please, don't be upset.'

'How could your chief know I had any books, since he has never visited my yacht?' I said scornfully.

He did not answer, put his head down and continued his work.

'Ah!' he suddenly said as I was dozing off. 'So, you are a photographer.'

'No' I said, 'but I take photographs.'

He held up a book. This particular book was written by a doctor friend in Cyprus, who used several of my photographs from the Arabian Gulf and Cyprus to illustrate a series of books he had written on the journeys of the great men found in the Bible and the Qur'an. This particular book was on the story of Abraham. I had no idea it was on board or that it included a credit to me. He then came to my many tourist maps of Spain. It was after two o'clock, and he had been here for three hours already. I was very tired and angry. Then I had an idea.

I went to the front cabin where Ghada was asleep and fumbled in the dark for my camera. Attaching the flash unit I switched it on, listening to the high-pitched whistle as the flash charged. I pressed the camera into Ghada's blanket to muffle the sound, hoping I would not wake her or alert the officer. The orange light illuminated: the batteries were charged and ready. I slowly turned to face the main saloon, pointed the lens in the direction of the officer and pressed the button.

There was a flash, followed by a loud scream.

He slammed down the map of Granada that was in his hand and shouted, 'Why did you do that?'

I was too stunned by his violent reaction to answer for a moment. 'I like to take photographs of my friends.'

'Give me the film,' he demanded, as he headed in my direction.

I refused to move and held the camera behind my back. He stood there in a rage, obviously not knowing what to do. I was shocked too, but determined not to hand over the camera.

He suddenly picked up all the sheets of paper he had written on, tore them to shreds, and threw them on the table. Anne and I looked on in amazement. Abruptly, he turned and marched up the steps of the companionway.

'I'll be back!' he shouted, 'I want that film!'

I sank down, totally exhausted and flabbergasted.

The incident has always remained a mystery. His concentrated efforts, for so many hours now seemed so worthless. It was essential for me to keep that photograph and I was sure that he would indeed return. In my chart table drawer, I found a new roll of film. Although the film in the camera was only half used, I rewound it, opened the back and removed it. I hid it above the chart table before placing the new roll in the camera.

Finally in bed, I was just dozing off, when there was a loud knock, closely followed by an assertive shout. Still drowsy, I could hear footsteps on the deck. I swung my legs over the side of the bunk, and hurriedly pulled on my trousers. The officer had returned.

'I have to have the film,' he said through clenched teeth.

Firmly, I explained that I would not give it to him.

'I will arrest you. It is illegal to take pictures of police officers,' he warned.

'OK. No problem. Arrest me, but you still will not get the film. This is my yacht and my film.'

He spotted my camera below on the chart table and I moved to block his way to prevent him from lunging for it. His tone changed.

'Please, Graham, give it to me. I will develop and return it to you tomorrow. I cannot: I will not, leave without it.'

'I'm sorry,' I said. 'I cannot give it to you. I don't trust developers here, they have ruined my films before, and I have some important photos on that roll.'

I wondered how long he would keep this up. It was now four o'clock, and I was exhausted. I guessed he was on duty all night.

After listening to more pleading, I finally agreed to hand over the film, and picked up my camera. Without rewinding, I opened the back and pulled out the film, winding several inches into the can between my finger and thumb. At the time, I thought an obviously exposed film was better than a blank film with no exposures, as there was no way he could tell if it had been the one I had used or not.

I handed him the film and he smiled as he promised to return it the next day. I trusted that after he saw the results, he would realize that I had exposed the film as I rewound it into the canister before his eyes, and so believe that I had destroyed the photograph of him. Over the following months I heard of several other yacht crews who also experienced the 'Midnight Books Incident'.

The speed humps in the road jolted me back to the present as we descended the slope into the marina. We parked and Mohammed came over to join us as we walked towards the yacht.

'Back already Graham?'

His tone sounded sarcastic. Suddenly, it hit me. This was the same policeman who had come to the yacht and demanded the camera. Now, he was the Chief of Police in the port! Shocked at this realization, I wondered what it meant. Was this revenge for taking his photograph and causing him to lose face? How else would he know my name? It was the same officer, of that I was sure.

I opened the yacht at the request of the officers. Mohammed and the two policemen came on board but did not immediately go below. They sat in the cockpit and asked if I had anything on board.

I told them wearily, 'Of course, I have many things on board.'

'Any guns, drugs, anything like that?' the chief, Mohammed, asked.

'Look Mohammed, you know me. I have been here many times before, and you know I do not have drugs or guns.'

He looked at me and whispered, 'Yes, I do know you, and know that you don't have these things.'

He spoke to the other officers and they all stood up to leave.

Fearing they may use the fact that the search was not done as an excuse to search later when I was not there, I said, 'Where are you going? Please, come below and take a look at my home!'

They agreed and I ushered them down below.

While the two officers looked around, without touching anything, Mohammed looked at the bookshelf; picked up a book, thumbed through the opening pages, and read the information on the title page. Any lingering doubts that it was him were now dispelled. 'Any more books?'

'Of course,' I said. 'Look, you can see there are many books. This is my home and I like to study.'

He cast a glance at me, while the other officers began to look under mattresses, cushions, and in cupboards.

Mohammed then asked, 'Any Bibles?' I pointed to one in Arabic on my bookshelf, as I answered, 'Yes, I am a Christian, of course I have Bibles.'

He smiled and said impatiently to his colleagues, '*Yallah*.'[1]

---

[1] Let's go.

3. The First Interrogation

Sunday 31st May 12.30pm

Once again, I locked the yacht and returned to the police van with the two officers. We immediately set off again in the direction of M'Diq. It was now past midday and the humidity hit me as we reached our destination. The doors opened and I stepped out of the van into the dusty yard of the police station, which still smelt heavily of diesel fumes. As I walked in, Jacques and the others were still sitting on the same plank of wood. Matti asked if all had gone well. I informed him that they had searched the yacht and found nothing.

Almost immediately we were taken back through the dim corridor into the same waiting van. The gates opened as the driver cheerily waved to the guards, and we set off in the direction of Tetouan, the provincial capital. The old *souk* or market place is very typically ancient Moroccan, but in a poor state compared with the older restored *souks* of other cities. Much of the architecture and layout of Tetouan is typically Spanish: a relic of not too distant colonial times.

Growing and processing marijuana, known locally as *kif*, has been a lucrative industry in this northern area of the country for centuries, especially higher up in the Rif, adding greatly to the wealth of the region. In spring, the humid morning air is often laden with the aroma of *kif*, which, wafted by the land breeze, carries it far out to sea.

We slowly passed through guarded, green-painted iron gates, which were opened as we approached. Over the shoulders of the officers in the front we could see a huge multi-storey block. It looked like one of those grim unpainted, concrete apartment buildings of the 1960s. We felt the van go down a steep incline below the level of the road and park in a yard. The rear doors opened. We had arrived at the police interrogation centre.

The officers conducted us through glazed doors and up three wide echoing flights of stairs. On the top land-ing we turned down a long corridor and were greeted by a large, friendly-looking man in a white open-necked shirt. A gun was tucked into his belt. Welcomes were exchanged between these men, before we were escorted by the larger of the two, into a room with a grey steel desk in the centre, and a wooden plank supported on a pile of bricks along one wall. Behind the desk, as in the police station, hung another huge picture of the King. Obviously once in colour, it was now reduced to a blue hue. The man beckoned us to sit down and then left. It was some time later before he returned with a short, thin man; both obviously police officers.

The short man carried a typewriter in his arms and placed it on the desk, before he began to search through the drawers for paper. There wasn't any. He left the room, returning with paper and carbon sheets. Silently, he slowly and carefully arranged them into five heaps, inserting one pile into the typewriter.

'*Parlez-vous Français?*' he asked, looking at me.

'No, English,' I replied.

Jacques said something to him and then looked towards me. I told Jacques that I did not want him to translate for us. Misunderstandings might take place. An interpreter who spoke my language fluently was essential, especially if there was to be the compilation of a police report, as I now suspected.

Everything appeared to move in slow motion, with no attempt by the officers to hurry. Would I make my appointment the following day with the Minister of Tourism in Rabat? I pondered, as I grew increasingly frustrated and impatient. Perhaps I could get the minister's assistance, if necessary, by phoning him in the morning. At least he could confirm to the police my reason for being in Morocco, as the meeting had been arranged months before.

It had been several years since I had first visited the minister, on the advice of a friend in Casablanca. He had seen the importance of having my book on the ports of North Africa accepted by the authorities. I agreed that it was an advantage to both of us. I would benefit from the information obtained from official government sources – charts and photographs – and the government would gain from the resulting tourism from the yachts that I would be assisting to sail to Morocco. There had been many changes of staff in the Ministry since I began the book, but I had always maintained the relationship with those in charge. The current director was as excited as I was to see the fulfilment of the project, and had already checked and accepted the draft text.

Earnestly seeking Jacques' attention, I repeated several times in different ways that he should request an interpreter, a lawyer, and contact with our ambassadors, as it seemed we were under arrest. The large officer laughed heartily when Jacques held his hands up and crossed his wrists.

'No, no arrest,' affirmed the officer looking at me. 'Friends. *Amigos!*' So began the first interrogation.

It was a friendly affair, as far as I could understand. The officer questioned first Jacques and then Françoise, asking for details relating to name, family, work, and relevant addresses. The whole process took a very long time. Correct spelling presented a problem, resulting in frequent stops and perpetual backspacing for the typist.

Finally it was my turn. The officer who was typing spoke no English. This did not stop him. Assisted by information from my passport and frequent referrals to what had been typed before during the interview with Jacques, information was documented. Information that we later discovered was incorrect.

I continued to protest that I wanted an interpreter, a lawyer and permission to phone my embassy.

'Not necessary,' the officer smiled, holding up his watch, now four o'clock in the afternoon. We would not be held for much longer, he inferred. We struggled on making little progress at communicating, until he suddenly got up and walked out of the room. Half an hour later he returned with a pretty young woman of around twenty years. She was dressed in traditional Moroccan dress, with a beige headscarf. The smell of henna, combined with the strong pungent odour of spices, blended with the scent in her clothes. It was a wonderful and welcome aroma coming into that bare smoke-filled room.

In beautiful English, she explained that the officer had pulled her off the street, and asked her to translate for us.

'I am a student at the university but I learned English at school.'

She apologized that she had not used it for some years, but would try to help us. I told her that I wanted a lawyer and to see my Consul, or at least phone my embassy, since we were apparently under arrest.

She spoke with the policeman and then said, 'No, he says you are not arrested. He just needs some details. This is only a formality and then you can go home.'

Since we had not been cautioned or handcuffed, I felt reassured.

The continual questioning was a slow process, taking well over an hour. Every answer I gave had to be translated, followed by an exchange between the two officers before typing could be resumed. Correct spelling continued to be a problem for the typist, with delays every few minutes as he back-spaced to correct a word. This tedious procedure involved lifting each page in turn, applying correcting fluid, then waiting for it to dry before repeating the procedure on the page beneath. The process was assisted by an officer blowing hard onto the papers.

The interrogator asked what I was doing in Morocco, how I had arrived, how often I had been before, whether I had visited any other countries, and then more personal details: my education, father's name, grandfather's name, nationality and occupation. He also wanted the names of my father's brothers and sisters. I had no idea! I had never met most of these relatives. The officer looked at me in disbelief, but I did not wish to tell him of my parents' separation when I was four years old, and my subsequent upbringing in a children's home. I had lived outside of the UK for much of my life.

The officer became more aggressive, obviously unconvinced that I did not know.

At one point he demanded: 'Are you a Jew? Is your family Jewish?'

I stopped listening. Slowly I straightened up and told him in a tone of exasperation, 'No I am not! These details cannot possibly have anything to do with my being here in the police station.' I then jokingly announced: 'I *can* remember the name of my grandfather's cat – if that is any help – Tibbles!'

There was silence as he stood looking perplexed, with his hands on his hips. Through the interpreter he then asked how it could possibly be that I knew the name of my grandfather's cat, but not his name.

Finally, he moved on to questions concerning my work and travels. I described my book and the co-operation I had been pleased to receive from the Ministries of Tourism in Morocco and Tunisia. Much later I discovered that no mention was made of this information in the reports compiled during this and subsequent inter-rogations, even though I had an appointment with a minister the following day.

At last, the relevant questions began.

'Why were you taking books to Jacques?'

'I was not taking books to Jacques,' I replied.

'Why did you have books on the yacht?'

'The yacht has been my home for many years, and because I am a teacher I quite naturally have many books.'

Shaking his head he responded, 'No one in Morocco has so many different books.'

'Why was he taking books to the Frenchman?' he asked, tossing his head in the direction of Matti.

I explained through the girl that Matti was taking a few Bibles to Jacques, who wanted to give them to friends who had requested them.

'It seemed perfectly reasonable to me,' I said. 'It is traditional to take a gift when visiting. Moroccans often give a copy of the Qur'an: I have been given many. Why would it be strange for a Christian to give a Bible?' I asked.

There was a lull in proceedings while the two officers were discussing what should be written in the report. My mind lapsed to the events of the previous evening that had precipitated our current plight. Jacques and Matti had a mutual friend who was delighted to hear that Matti had decided to re-visit Morocco with me. Once we had arrived and off-loaded my motor scooter from the yacht, Matti immediately asked to go for a ride around the marina on it. He zipped around the port several times before finding Jacques' apartment. He visited him the following day, and then decided to deliver the gift he had brought him in the evening. This is when the trouble began.

The port consists of a large complex of shops and apartments, as well as several police and military posts: one was located right outside Jacques' apartment. The apartments are accessed via manned barriers, each with a guard or a policeman, ready to lift the pole at the approach of vehicles.

Matti had been riding around but had not interacted with the men at the barriers – only demanded their opening. On this occasion the young man asked him for a packet of cigarettes. Telling the fellow he did not smoke, Matti carried on under the lifted barrier pole. His refusal sparked the crisis we now faced. This time he had been carrying a small black bag with some books inside.

The man at the barrier was indignant at Matti's refusal to part with a gift of cigarettes, so he informed the police that he was carrying something. I am sure at this stage there was no suspicion. The fellow just wanted what he saw as his due reward for lifting the barrier several times throughout the day for this crazy foreigner tearing around on a motor scooter. As Matti slowed at the next barrier, he was again asked for cigarettes. He became angry, shaped by his previous bad experience in Morocco. He turned round in disgust and sped back along the road.

As he returned, he was told to stop again. He refused, not realizing who had asked him, or why. He had no way of knowing that almost everyone in the marina was a policeman. A chase ensued as he drove off towards the yacht, with the chief of police following behind in his Ford Capri. Even then, Matti was enjoying the fun, totally unaware of the trouble he had caused. Finally his bag was searched, and a small number of books – Bibles – were discovered. Matti later admitted that he was uncooperative, since he did not know these people were policemen: 'I did not believe that I had done anything wrong.' His belligerence only made matters worse.

It seemed almost unbelievable that such a seemingly minor event could lead to five people having to explain their life history and having it translated into Arabic.

'How did you come to know Jacques?' the officer asked.

I explained that the work on my book brought me on many visits to Morocco and that I had often met Jacques in the marina, where he rented an apartment.

'He was the only foreigner there and I would meet him for coffee.' The marina was en route south to Rabat, where I often visited government officials.

Jacques was retired and loved the peaceful life of the port. He and Françoise had moved here from another marina further along the coast, when noise became a problem in summer. Much of their time was spent travelling around the countryside enjoying the peace and tranquillity offered by the contrasting lifestyle of the people in this beautiful country.

I insisted that no crime had been committed. Matti had given Christian books to Jacques, a Frenchman. No Moroccan nationals had been involved. I later discovered that the friendly exchange with the officer was a mistake. By twisting my responses, my answers generated fictitious ideas that were recorded onto the paper and subsequently used to convict me. In this instance, my replies were contorted into a false confession stating that we came to distribute books and to corrupt Moroccans.

I went on to tell the officer that the prophet Mohammed encouraged his followers to read the Christian Scriptures.[1] Rather than try to argue a case, I liked to tell anyone wanting to know more about what Christians believed to simply read the Bible: the basis of our faith.

The interrogation continued and the typist laboriously hammered away. Suddenly the girl stopped interpreting, stood up and said she had to leave. Her parents were waiting for her and they would be anxious. The officers tried to convince her to stay longer, but she pleaded with them to allow her to depart. I thanked her for her diligence, and she left. The officer appeared to have finished with me and went off in search of another translator for Matti and Veikko. The remaining officer seemed grateful for the break from the typewriter, and immediately lit up a cigarette.

Matti spoke English with a strong Finnish accent, and with almost no hint of his adopted Canadian homeland. His speech developed into a distinctive stutter when he was nervous. Veikko's English differed little to my ears from the Finnish he spoke with Matti when they chatted together.

The officer returned without a translator, unable to persuade anyone else in off the street. He proceeded to open the passports, and to identify each of us before he came to Matti's. As he opened it, he spelled out his name for the typist. His attempts to talk with Matti failed,

---

[1] Most Muslims have many misguided ideas about what Christians believe.

despite his willingness to co-operate. There were long periods when the officer was talking to the typist, obviously telling him what to write. I wondered what he was saying about Matti and Veikko, as he was constantly referring to and copying sections from my typed answers. At least there were less typing mistakes occurring now!

Matti seemed surprisingly keen to co-operate. I could see that he, too, was concerned about the amount of typing going on. Veikko just sat back, almost asleep.

At one point, Matti was asked if he had brothers and sisters. He told the officer he had a sister, who had died in tragic circumstances. From the boredom of the routine questioning, the officer's eyes lit up and he became excited, asking many questions through Jacques about this.

'How old was she, where she was living at the time? How long ago, how did she die?'

Matti became increasingly upset with each question, many of which were repeated several times in different ways, in order to be understood. He began to weep as he was forced to recall the circumstances. The officer continued, showing no sympathy whatsoever.

I intervened, putting my hand on Matti's shoulder, 'Matti, don't tell him anything more. This has nothing to do with the police and our present situation.'

It was several more hours before we were finally finished. The officer collected up the papers and placed them in five neat piles, removing the black carbon copy sheets. He looked at Jacques and held out a pen expectantly. After a brief exchange Jacques signed where shown, followed by Françoise. As they returned to their seats the officer held out the pen to me. I walked over to the desk and picked up the papers indicated as mine. I studied the faint, closely typed Arabic script and I could not even attempt to decipher any of it without my glasses, which were on the yacht.

I turned to Jacques and asked him, 'What's this? What are we being asked to sign?'

Jacques shrugged his shoulders.

'I have no intention of signing anything I do not understand!' I told him.

Then the police officer spoke quietly with Jacques.

'We cannot be released without signing the papers,' Jacques said.

'But we have no idea what has been recorded on them,' I pointed out. 'For the past half hour the officer has been typing without us even talking! How could we possibly know what he had typed? It is all in Arabic!'

Jacques did not appear to have any comprehension of what I was telling him and just stared ahead.

'Are you so convinced we are about to be released?' I asked.

'*Oui, Oui,*' he replied softly.

Ignoring my refusal, the officer proceeded to call Veikko and Matti over, pointing the pen in their direction. Veikko took the pen from his outstretched hand and stood there looking at Matti, unsure what to do. I explained again why I thought we should not sign. Veikko looked pleadingly at me and complained that he felt ill and needed to get back to the yacht. He would sign if Matti thought he should, he indicated. Matti began to stutter and looked pitiful.

'You have to decide for yourselves.' I told them. 'I will not sign under any circumstances without knowing what is written.'

Veikko and Matti signed, following the example of Jacques and Françoise.

The officer again held out the pen in my direction. I took it and placed it on top of the paper, but without writing anything. The officer ignored this and took up the papers, placing a clip in the corner of each. He spoke to Jacques, and left the room. Although I read at the top of the papers the words in heavy black type, in French: '*Procès Verbal*',[2] I had no idea what that meant. I was to become very familiar with this document, or at least, with the one that succeeded it.

I asked Jacques what the officer had said prior to leaving the room.

'Everything is good,' he said. He had been reassured that we had done nothing that would keep us here. I guessed this could be true, since we had not been charged, and the atmosphere was quite friendly throughout most of the questioning. I sighed with relief that our ordeal was over. It had taken the whole day. Under no supervision now and feeling greatly relieved, we wandered around the room for a while and soon ventured out into the corridor.

An hour later, the two officers returned.

'You have to wait for the boss,' the larger one told us.

I asked Jacques to tell him that we would like some food. It was late in the evening and we were hungry and thirsty, as we had not even been given anything to eat or drink all day. Jacques relayed this and the two officers spoke together. An argument broke out. After some minutes the larger officer left the room, after indicating to Jacques that he would see what he could do. The other officer remained with us. Jacques patiently tried to converse with him, but it seemed he did not communicate well.

Believing that the ordeal would soon be over, I began to talk to the remaining officer, in the Lebanese Arabic I

---

[2] A police statement based on the questions asked by the police and the answers given.

knew. I discovered he was from a small town at the foot of the Rif Mountains called Al Hociema. I had been there the previous year, to take photographs of the port for my book.

I began to converse with him in Spanish, which he knew well. *'Que pasa?'* I asked him. He did not really know what was happening, but from what he gathered, we had not committed any offence.

'El problema es la aduana.'

'The problem is with the customs authorities,' he said. It was months before I understood the full significance of this comment.

'Surely,' I pressed, 'if no offence has been committed, we should not be detained here.'

He informed me that we would soon be out, as it all seemed to be a mistake. Reassured, I relaxed a little and immediately felt hungry. I tried to decide which of the restaurants we should visit.

It was more than half an hour before the officer returned.

Impatiently, he stated, 'You have to wait here longer, before you can be released.'

Through Jacques, I again told him we were hungry, and had not eaten or even been given water for the entire day. He again broke into an argument with his colleague, followed by more shouting and gesticulating. Finally he stomped towards the door, beckoning us to follow.

We hurried down the stairs and up the incline to the gates through which we had entered many hours earlier. He spoke with the officers guarding the gates. They were obviously taken from a military detachment, as they were dressed in smart fatigues and berets and carried automatic rifles slung across their shoulders. The officer whisked us out into the street. It was very late evening and humid. The smell of meat cooking on charcoal hung in the air, along with the smell of poor drainage. It smelt good: it was the smell of freedom after many hours confined in a small room.

We were led into a crowded café a few streets away and stood at the counter. The officer tried to tell us what they offered, but we were not familiar with the names of anything he mentioned. He ordered six sandwiches and glasses of orange juice, which were delivered almost immediately.

The greasy chicken rolls spiced with chilli were wrapped in paper, which we peeled back. After only a few minutes he looked at his watch and said: '*Yallah*' (let's go). Hurriedly we ate but it was difficult, as the rolls tasted spicier in a dry mouth, and on an empty stomach. Although still hungry, I did not ask for more, believing we would soon be released. Later, I wished that I had at least purchased a bottle of water.

The officer asked me to pay. We then made our way quickly back up the hill to the steel gates, down the ramp and through the glazed doors to the stairwell, returning to the same room as before. The big officer left, but soon returned, sweating profusely and beckoning us to follow him. He led the way up another flight of stairs to a wide landing above, and stood outside a door for several minutes before it opened.

An ugly-looking man dressed in a suit came out and looked at us, scowling and breathing deeply through a cigarette clenched firmly between his teeth. He said nothing and retreated back inside with the two officers. After a few more minutes the door re-opened and the officers emerged and walked towards the stairwell, indicating for us to follow. I asked Jacques what was happening. He spoke to the officer, who apparently replied that we had to be taken to the cells.

I stopped dead and shouted, 'Why?'

The officers, who were already several steps below me, returned to the place where I was standing and explained to Jacques how sorry they were.

The big one said, 'There is no alternative. You have to come down. Follow me.'

I was angry with myself for not taking any of the opportunities that had arisen throughout the day to use my mobile phone to warn Anne or someone that we were in trouble. The truth is that up until this point, I had no idea we were in trouble. My phone had been turned off all day to conserve the battery. I had been surprised that we had not been asked if we had mobile phones. Believing that we were not actually under arrest had been my stronghold throughout the day. It now seemed I was wrong. And this was just the beginning. Everything around me was about to change. My life would never be the same again.

4. Down to the Dungeon

Sunday 31st May 11pm

It was late at night when we were led along a corridor and down several flights of stairs to the basement of the interrogation centre. The building was huge, with six floors and many rooms leading from each of the corridors we passed, before reaching the next flight of stairs. A lot of the doors were open allowing us to see inside some of them. Apart from a cheap grey office desk with a steel tubular or wooden rush-seated chair, most rooms were unfurnished.

Several of the offices also contained the familiar plank of wood along one wall, resting on a pile of bricks. Other rooms were heaped high from floor to ceiling with old files, balanced precariously on top of metal filing cabinets. I wondered why they needed so many similar rooms. Surely there could not possibly be that many felons in this town? The building felt empty, perhaps because it was Sunday.

There was an echo as we descended the wide, grey, dimly lit stairwell. For the first time I began to feel the cold chill of fear creep up my neck. My legs felt weak. Since we had entered the building that morning, we had been on one of the upper floors, undergoing intensive interrogation. Having consumed only one glass of orange and a roll during the past twelve hours or so had not concerned me. Now though, the lack of fluids and the sustained tension throughout the day was affecting me. It felt rather like stepping off a roller coaster, a feeling that was to become all too familiar over the next few months.

I had been almost unconcerned until now, even to some extent enjoying the challenge of this new experience. We had done nothing against either the civil or Islamic law, I was sure.

Just a little smug that I had got away without signing that document myself, I wondered what the effect of the other signatures might be on all of us. In my naivety, I never considered the possibility that my friends could be – indeed had been – pressed into signing a document in Arabic that incriminated me in a subversion plot against the Kingdom of Morocco: a plot to overthrow the government, no less.

A concern as we continued the slow walk down to the basement was the way in which questions were addressed to me. I was assumed to be the leader, even though nothing had been found on me, or aboard my yacht. Was it simply because I was the captain and had offered to shoulder responsibility? Even this seemed odd, as I had no connection with Jacques and Françoise, even if I, as captain, had taken responsibility for the Canadians. In an Arab culture, the eldest person is always the one addressed and afforded the respect as leader. Jacques was a good many years older than I was.

As we continued our descent, I began to wonder if this was all a dream. After all, the fat policeman had been so friendly and had insisted, throughout the day, that we were not under arrest and would soon be released. How could our fortunes have changed so rapidly to the point that we were now on our way to the cells to be more permanently incarcerated? Surely he knew the situation? After all, he did keep shaking his head, saying he did not know why we were here. Was it all an act? Was he just trying to show empathy for us, while knowing exactly what was going on?

We reached the bottom of the building, and were led across a courtyard and through the underground car park of the interrogation centre. As the night air wafted across my face, I was again aware of several different smells: drains, poor sewage and dampness were the strongest. Doubts and fears swept over me, amplifying the humid night air, and, despite the chill, bringing on a sweat. For the first time, I began to wonder if the police had found some grounds for holding us.

We could not easily communicate with our inter-rogators, and I now worried as to what exactly could have been written on those many pages of typed Arabic, which the others had signed. If the fat policeman was not as genuine as he had pretended to be, we may have 'confessed' to anything. What had we said that could justify being held, I wondered?

We arrived at the basement and I asked the officers again if we could have something to eat and some water, indicating with my hands what I wanted. No reply. I repeated the request in Arabic, thinking that nothing would be lost at this stage, but still no response.

We were led into a large bricked-up underground basement with half-opened, green painted metal sliding doors. Once inside, the smell and feel of the damp were pervasive. At the far end a tall uniformed officer sat behind a grey metal desk, scribbling into a large book. I could see a pile of passports on the desk. He did not look up. There was an iron fence with a heavy metal gate stretching the entire length of the basement. Through the

Local village scene, Tetouan province.

bars I could see that the gate led to an alleyway. We could hear muffled shouting on the other side of the wall, coming from the alleyway, where I could see the cell doors stretching down the corridor. I refused to contemplate going through the gate.

A heap of dirty, dark brown blankets lay at the far end of the huge room we were entering. We were ushered in and motioned to stay there, as the officers retreated back through the doors, slid them almost closed and departed into the blackness. There was no furniture and we hesitated to squat down on the cold concrete floor, so we stood there. At first, we huddled together at the end nearest the entrance, wondering what was to happen next. Were we to stay here all night? Too numbed to speak and beginning to shiver, I still felt it was my responsibility to keep up our morale.

After several minutes the officer was still seated behind his desk; engrossed in writing. We began to relax, thinking that perhaps they would leave us here, rather than take us deeper inside to the cells. We talked optimistically about the day's interrogation, and felt some reassurance from the words that had been repeated many times throughout the day: 'You have done nothing wrong and are not accused of any crime. This is simply a customs offence, a minor indiscretion.' Were we about to be released? Was the officer filling in our passport details, about to return them to us?

Suddenly the officer stood up. Scraping his chair on the concrete, he beckoned to us to come towards the table. As we neared the desk, he tried to communicate something to me. I knew he wanted us to give our names, but I made no visible sign that I understood, while mentally trying to work out why he needed them, since he held our passports in his hand. Jacques translated that he wanted our names, and I told him to tell the officer that he had our passports, and could work it out for himself. I was beginning to feel angry and upset at our circumstances.

The officer looked at me as he sat down again, and began to write in the columns of his huge book. I could not help but be reminded of those large ledgers I had seen in Dickens' films, as he copied our names from the passports. Once again I wondered why I was the one addressed and not Jacques. I deduced that they considered me to be the spokesman, even though I did not speak French or Moroccan Arabic. But then how would this officer know anything about us?

After he had written our names, he went over to the metal cabinets, pulled out a tray containing several small steel boxes, and told us to empty the contents of our pockets into the boxes. Slowly, we complied. He noted how much cash we handed over. I wondered if there was some way to keep my mobile phone, but realized it would not work down here, and that the battery would soon be flat. Reluctantly, I placed it in the tray. Too late, I realized that I should have removed and concealed the tiny electronic SIM card. At least if the phone handset was stolen, it could not then have been used with my account.

Satisfied that our pockets were empty, he ordered us to remove our belts and shoelaces. I felt another rush of cold sweat and knew for sure that we were on our way to the cells. I began to prepare myself for this by contemplating the closed, barred, iron gate and what lay beyond. From this angle I could see more of the long, dimly lit corridor, with many darkened doors along it. I thought of that frightening cell at the police station in M'Diq. Apart from becoming aware of a few groans from deep inside, the place seemed very quiet. That gave me some comfort. I wondered how many people could be housed in there.

Once stripped of our possessions, belts and shoelaces, the officer sat down at his desk again, and began to fill in a space beside each name in his ledger. He entered details in the book after examining the contents of the trays, which each now contained a small piece of paper that recorded our names. While we awaited our inevitable fate, I tried to imagine the place where we were to be taken. I knew it would be a shock, but one that I hoped could be lessened by mental visualization. I tried to envisage the worst, hoping to minimize my fear. Surely a dark, cold cell with steel bunk beds stacked two or three high against a wall, each with dirty mattresses, and a bucket at the end of the cell. Then there would be the smell.

I continued to prepare myself mentally for the next step as we walked towards the iron gate. Then I noticed for the first time a plastic bucket just to the right of the gate, and wandered towards it, feeling nervous as I approached. I wanted to convince myself that I wasn't scared. I recalled the words of Mohammed before we left the marina: 'Be brave Graham, be strong.' He must have known exactly what would transpire.

A pungent, strange and sweet odour got stronger as I edged closer to the bucket. I forced myself to take a look inside. It was half full of a brown liquid into which potato and orange peel had been thrown. A sweet smell of overripe fruit reached my nostrils. There were white maggots or similar creatures crawling over the top, across the peelings. Later, I learned that this bucket was the food for the entire cell block.

After half an hour the officer finished writing and stood up. He pulled a large bunch of keys from his pocket, allowing them to dangle on a string securely tied around his waist, and walked towards the gate. Before opening it, he once again frisked each of us to ensure our pockets were empty. I was relieved that I had handed over my mobile phone. He was sure to have found it as he patted me down, right where I would have tried to conceal it.

The officer reached for the string around his waist, hauling up the bunch of huge iron keys. One of them was inserted into the lock of the gate. Deliberately trying to occupy my mind, I thought how ironic it was that in our technological society, the ancient symbol of the jailer with his large bunch of rusty keys, complete with a ring onto which they were all attached, was not so obsolete after all.

He swung the gate open and ushered us through without closing it behind him. I counted eight massive steel doors lining both sides of the corridor beyond. Each had a small grille two-thirds of the way up. At the far end was another door, and I could just make out a black, shiny face peering through the grille. We would soon become familiar with that cell.

The jailer peered through the grille of the first cell door on the left, before rummaging through his bunch of keys and inserting one into the lock. He flung the door open and looked inside. In the dim light projected from the corridor, I could see that blood was splattered on the wall and a lifeless form lay on the floor. He pushed his foot against the body, which rocked a little and groaned. The door was closed with a huge echoing slam. He passed to the next cell.

The second door revealed another dark room with splashes of blood on the walls. Apart from a dark, crumpled heap of blankets in the centre of the concrete floor, it was empty. He went inside and backed out again, before closing the door. As he did so, a pungent sickly odour escaped. He skipped the next door, where we could see the dark faces of two women, peering out through the bars, their heads covered with a scarf. We were led to the fourth door.

After inserting the key to unlock the door, the jailer looked in, and then shoved all the men inside: Jaques, Matti, Veikko and me. He held back Françoise, grabbing her firmly by the arm. She shrieked and Jacques protested, letting out a shout. As he did so, the massive iron door swung shut with a loud metallic squeak of the hinges, followed by an almighty clank that seemed to make the whole building reverberate for several seconds. It was a sound that will haunt me for the rest of my life; a sound I will never forget.

5. Inside the Cell

Monday 1st June 1.30am

We listened intently to hear what the jailer was planning to do with Françoise, and for the first time I became aware of shouting and banging from further along the corridor. Jacques strained at the grille and shouted to Françoise, who responded in a terrified high-pitched voice. When another door opened, we presumed that Françoise had been found a cell. We later learned that she had been placed with one other woman.

Our surroundings were bleak indeed. Even imagining the worst had not prepared me for this. It was cold and I began to shiver uncontrollably. As my eyes grew accustomed to the gloom, it became clear there was nothing at all in the cell – no furniture, no beds, no mattresses – just a cold, damp concrete floor, sloping gently down towards a hole at the far end to the left. This was the toilet, I assumed. There was a short stub of pipe projecting above this hole, and a trickle of water fell noisily to the floor, creating a splash that added to the chill. Through the gloom I could see that the walls were bare rough concrete, as was the ceiling.

The cell was two metres wide and some four metres long. As I was absorbing our new surroundings in the dim light, I heard footsteps outside. The jailer returned, opened the door, and pushed Jacques out of the way. A shaft of light appeared as he threw in four blankets. A cloud of dust was illuminated in the light, as they fell to the floor. I asked him for water, and he pointed with a grimace towards the hole at the far end of the cell.

As he closed the door with another noisy, echoing creak and a clank, the other inmates further along began to shout and bang on their cell doors. We did not know what the commotion was about, but the activity was terrifying. It became even more sinister when the human voices stopped, but the strange echoing metallic noises continued. It took some minutes to settle down. We said nothing to each other as we each picked up a blanket, all feeling equally nervous and unsettled by the noise.

Jacques pressed his head against the grille and shouted to Françoise. We could hear her faint, frightened voice, as she responded. He was able to converse with her a little, and then began to whistle and sing, gently encouraging her with his soft French tones. It was very moving. I wondered how, at his age, he had so much energy, considering the deprivations of the day.

We all stood near the door, 'hanging on' to the little shaft of dim light that passed though the grille past Jacques' head. We were unwilling to venture down in the direction of the blackness, and to the hole at the end. I shook my blanket and, although I could not see it, I could feel and smell dust and grit, some of which went into my eyes. There was also a musty smell of mould. Each of us pulled our blanket around our shoulders and began to squat along one side of the cell, propping ourselves up against the wall. There was just enough room for all of us along the length of it, leaving a reasonable distance to the water pipe and the hole.

I thanked God that here at least there was not the pungent odour which had emanated from the other cells we had looked into, but only the smell of urine. We did not have a problem with the hole, and soon got used to the smell. Jacques said goodnight to Françoise through the grille, sank down on his haunches to join us, and began to sing a hymn softly. We joined in although I did not know the words – quietly at first and then louder, for the sake of Françoise, who we could hear accompanying us. We then stood up and prayed quietly together for strength, arms across each other's shoulders, in a tight circle. It felt good to be together.

I guessed it was around two o'clock in the morning, and we had been up for most of the previous night also. All my muscles were aching with tiredness and from the tension of the day. We began to stretch out; my feet were just about touching the opposite wall. Soon we found it necessary to stay close to each other in order to keep warm. Although it felt good to be horizontal, the dampness of the concrete floor soon penetrated through the flimsy fabric of our clothes.

It was impossible to relax and it took time for each of us to find the best way to use our blankets, which were thin, rotting and smelly. The slightest tug started a rip along the weft. It seemed best to use their dubious qualities as an insulator from the damp floor, rather than as a cover. Eventually, I folded mine four times, in an effort to get the largest coverage with the maximum thickness.

I was thankful that we had set off early in the morning and that I had thought to wear jeans and a jumper, despite the expected heat of the day. Throughout the sleepless night I tried every combination of position and blanket shape, but it was too cold and too damp to sleep. The hardness of the floor was the biggest problem. It brought back memories of the only other time that I had slept on a concrete floor. It had been in the south of Lebanon, in the early 1980s, soon after the Israeli invasion, when I was working as a volunteer with World Vision. I was part of a small team helping Palestinians rebuild their homes in a town that had been bombed by the Israelis. All the men of the village had been captured and killed by the Israeli ground troops, or had fled, leaving the villages helpless and the women and children without shelter. Only the very old men were left.

The cold was intense now that we were still. Each time I turned over it was a long struggle before my legs would follow. The occasional snoring, coming from Jacques, was somehow comforting. We did not talk during the night, realizing that any level of sleep was much needed. The way we said 'good night' to one another was rather ironic, as if we were sharing a room in a hotel. I tried to pretend that we were. I could not help thinking wistfully of my bed on the yacht. Occasionally I managed to doze off, only to be awoken by the pain of the hard floor pressing on my bones.

No amount of trying to think myself into a soft bed lasted for long. The most comfortable position was on my stomach, although my pelvic bones touched the floor, and the chill through the blanket was soon unbearable. I developed a routine of spending about ten minutes in each position and then rolling over, attempting to maintain each arrangement for as long as possible. I had broken my shoulder not long before, in a motor-cycle accident in Spain, so lying on one side was particularly painful.

The image of those bloodstained cells, which we had seen on the way to this one, was a harsh reminder of what our captors were capable of. I kept straining to hear noises that might indicate that it was morning, or that the guard was coming. It amazed me how the lack of sleep and visual sensory deprivation led to a need to hear something – anything new and different. It concerned me that we had only been captive for one day and night. How would I cope with several days or possibly months? An involuntary shudder went through me, as I forced myself to think about other things.

I began to think about Matti, who was lying next to me and nearest the hole. I had a mixture of feelings towards him. Why had he ignored my advice not to take the books to Jacques? Arab Muslims always seem to think that any night-time activity is suspicious, or at the very least, inauspicious. I realized that Matti would not have known why I had advised such caution, and we both knew that he was doing nothing illegal.

I could not help but feel admiration for the way he was coping with our new situation. I knew how terrified he was and could feel his tremors. I was concerned that he seemed unable to talk about it, being paralysed by fear. I knew too, that if he began to voice his fears, he would be unable to stop himself breaking down completely. His stutter had got markedly worse and he now had difficulty speaking at all. I wondered how deeply he was affected by re-living the trauma of his sister's death, and whether to talk with him about this later, to try to help him deal with it.

My mind flashed back to the moment when I first saw him after his arrest. Handcuffed, his face had lost its colour and he looked terrified, yet he kept up the pretence of defiance and continued to demand his rights. It was a pitiful sight. I thought how closely he had come to fulfilling his mission. All he had wanted to do was to see that Jacques received his books.

Although in his early forties, he looked very young and was full of boyish energy. A 'young, rich kid', he had made a considerable amount of money as a result of the development and sale of a company manufacturing large industrial cranes. Later, when he already had a fortune, he won a huge lottery prize. He never seemed to me to be the type of person who could manage such wealth. He was an outgoing guy, more interested in adventure than astute management of finances. Wonderfully innocent, it seemed to me; but then I hardly knew him.

It was an effort to try to think only good thoughts towards him, while suppressing my deeper anger with him for landing us here. I felt it was his naivety, perhaps stupidity that had got us into this mess. I wondered if his acceptance of the situation, which was out of character with his nature, was because he felt guilty, or was it because he was just too terrified to react? He even volunteered to sleep nearest the hole in the floor. Perhaps he had not realized that it was there or not known what it was.

During that long night, I recalled reading in the Spanish Press about a Moroccan who had been imprisoned and beaten savagely for declaring that he was a Christian. The evidence used against him was that he had a Bible. I wondered if he was still languishing in some prison, and felt somewhat proud to identify myself with him.

I wondered if the problem existed in Morocco because it was a secular Islamic state. Perhaps, they really did not know what Mohammed taught, whereas people of the fundamentalist states were educated in these teachings. Was this the reason for the difficulties that Christians faced here: a genuine ignorance of what the Qur'an says about Christians and their beliefs? After all, the Prophet had encouraged his followers to read the *Tawrat*, *Zabur* and *Injil*: the Old Testament, Psalms and New Testament, as recorded in the Qur'an. He had a great respect for

Christians, even calling them 'The People of the Book'. It is obvious from the Qur'an and the writings of the Hadith[1] that he gained much religious insight from the Christians he met and conversed with.

Many of the biblical stories, written several hundred years before, are repeated in the Qur'an, albeit often with some details transposed.[2] It is thought by many that it was because of Mohammed's disgust with some Christians who did not, in his eyes, truly follow or practise their faith, that he founded his own religion, based on the principles of monotheism.[3]

Why were the authorities so afraid of a book that Mohammed quoted from so liberally? I knew the arguments usually presented, and took the opportunity, this long, dark, uncomfortable night, to rehearse them in my mind, in case I needed them.

Many years ago I wanted to take a Moroccan friend who had been very hospitable to me to see the ancient Anglican church building in Tanger. He was forbidden entry by the Moroccan door-keeper, who informed us that it was illegal for him to even enter the premises and that he would be arrested if he tried to do so. Although it seemed difficult to believe, any Moroccan who declared his true faith if it was not Islam could be imprisoned. I had read that the constitutional right to religious tolerance and freedom was interpreted narrowly as 'the right to practice Islam'.

---

[1] Traditional interpretations of the sayings of Mohammad by Islamic scholars.

[2] For example the stories of the life of Abraham, the sacrifice of Isaac and the birth and life of Jesus.

[3] Many Muslims are confused about what Christians believe because of the way we express one God in three forms: God the Father, Son and Holy Spirit.

It was some comfort to know that the situation we were in could be worthwhile and develop into a mission with a purpose, even if it was an involuntary one. I felt myself forgiving Matti, and feeling a deep compassion and warmth towards him. I also prayed silently for Françoise, whose physical frailty would be tested in these early hours.

6. The Second Interrogation

Monday 1st June 5am

It had been an agonizing and sleepless night. At last I could see a faint, yellowish glow merging with the dim light of the electric lamp in the corridor, shining through the small grille in the door. I tried to figure out how any daylight could get through, since we were underground. There must be a ventilation shaft above the corridor, I guessed. Certainly there were no windows down here. The noise of other prisoners groaning and shouting from further along the corridor confirmed that morning had arrived. I attempted to work out what time it must be by trying to remember what time the dawn had broken on previous days.

We heard a guard unlocking and opening the gate. We lay wide awake listening to his footsteps, but did not move. He walked towards our cell, passed it, but then entered another one further along. We began to stir but did not get up. There was a scuffle outside the cell, and some shouting. Again, the thought of the blood-stained cells which we had seen the night before came to mind. I knew it was common for prisoners to be severely beaten, and wondered if we were about to witness such an event. It was very unusual for this to happen to foreigners –

white ones anyway – but was often carried out in close proximity, in order to intimidate them.

Acquaintances in the marinas of Spain had reported this to me. Many had first-hand experience as a result of their involvement in the marijuana trade.

I warned the others of what might occur next, but immediately realized that just voicing this fear made me tremble. I wished I had said nothing, as a feeling of helplessness came over me. It was a relief to hear the people, whoever they were, move away through the gate without incident.

Several hours passed with very little activity, apart from shouting and banging by other prisoners. I wondered if breakfast would be brought and if so, what. Stale bread? Perhaps a cup of water? Would it be edible, I wondered, or lead to chronic diarrhoea? No need to have worried; nothing came. None of us dared drink the water coming from the pipe.

Finally we heard the key in the lock and our door was flung open. The guard beckoned us out. Jacques immediately took his arm and asked where Françoise was being held. The guard assured him that she was here. We were led out along the corridor to the iron gate, where Françoise was standing, looking shrivelled and even more frail than usual. Did we all look so awful after just one day without food and water, and one night in the cells? This could go on for months if they decided to detain us.

As I was contemplating the worst, the guard hailed us over to the desk with the book. He opened the drawer, removed another bunch of keys, and went over to the row of steel cabinets. The trays containing our possessions were then withdrawn. My heart leapt at the thought that we were about to be released. Smiles appeared on all our faces, as we excitedly replaced belts and filled our pockets with our few possessions.

It was a relief to see my mobile phone. I turned it on, and noticed that the screen indicated 'no signal'. Quickly I turned it off again to conserve the battery. I breathed a sigh of relief that I had not tried to secrete it away the previous night, with all the consequences that could have incurred had it been discovered. I counted my cash: it was all there.

Two more guards were now in the basement. 'Find out what's happening!' I told Jacques.

We were to be taken upstairs, he discovered. I wondered what that meant, and chose to think that we were about to be released. During the night I had wondered if the two policemen who had interviewed us were amateurs, perhaps the weekend staff. This was the only reason I could think of to explain why the building was so empty. Perhaps the real 'professionals', the week-day workers were here now, and had recognized what a dreadful mistake the weekenders had made during their absence.

We were asked to sign the book, presumably to acknowledge that our possessions had been returned. As we were ushered out, I noticed a large fat man, dressed in the traditional white, one-piece *dish dash*, the dress of the Gulf Arabs. He was wearing the same type of sandals as mine, which I had purchased in Cyprus some years before when I lived there. Cyprus had been a base for my yacht for ten years, and my children had been educated there. I greeted him with a typical Gulf Arabic expression. He looked up and grunted: '*Salam Alikhum*'[1] in response, but not with a Gulf accent.

---

[1] 'Peace be with you'. This is a standard greeting used in North Africa and most Gulf States.

As we walked along I breathed deeply, taking in the air and enjoying the feeling of freedom. I could now see that this was an open courtyard, where the police vans were protected from the blazing sun except when it was directly overhead. The large room from which we had emerged through the sliding doors was obviously the original underground car park. We went through the glazed door of the main building and began ascending the stairs.

We had not eaten a meal for over thirty hours – probably nearer forty, since we did not have breakfast the morning the police came for us, and I was beginning to feel very thirsty. My voice sounded several pitches higher than usual, and I tried to lower it but without success. The police officer told us to keep quiet, as we slowly made our way up the stairs, which was crowded with people going in both directions.

On the third floor we were led into a room with a grey steel desk in the centre, a plank of wood fixed to the wall, and a door leading off to another room. There was no other furniture apart from two chairs. A large faded picture of the King looked benevolently down from behind the desk, as in most rooms. We were ordered to sit on the plank and wait. Another desk was brought in and placed beside the first one. A plain-clothes officer brought in a typewriter and dumped it noisily on the desk, seating himself behind it. After some minutes of waiting, I stood up and asked for water. My request was ignored. I then produced some money from my pocket, but the man pointed to the bench, indicating for me to sit down. This was a bad omen. It did not look as if we were going to be released after all. I had to try to telephone Anne.

I indicated to one of the officers that I wanted to visit the toilet. He understood and led me out along the corridor. I beckoned Jacques and Matti to follow me, and as we went along, I explained quietly what I intended to do. While walking behind me, they engaged the officer in conversation.

The toilet was an open hole-in-the-ground affair with a short door. I prayed that no one else would come in and squatted down so that my head could not be seen if anyone entered. I heard Jacques and Matti talking loudly outside, trying to hide the sound of my voice as I talked on the phone. I turned it on and waited. To my delight there was a signal. I dialled home in Spain and prayed for a reply. I heard the ringing tone, followed by the clicks of a connection, as Anne picked it up.

'We are in big trouble,' I began. 'I really do not know how deep or exactly why. Phone the British Embassy in Rabat and other friends to let them know. We are in the police station in Tetouan. I can't say more as my battery is low and I may need it again.'

Anne acknowledged and we disconnected. I breathed a sigh of relief, turned off the phone and replaced it back on its clip on my belt, hiding it under my pullover. As I was about to open the door, I wondered if I ought to use the toilet in case there was no other opportunity, but the thought made me aware of the terrible smell, which in my excitement, I had not noticed. I never got used to the smell of toilets, especially in restaurants in the Middle East and North Africa. Matti went in for a few seconds, before emerging having come to the same conclusion, and we returned to the room.

After waiting for half an hour, a short, thin man strode in, gesticulating wildly. He was dressed in an ill-fitting, shabby, black suit. He shouted loudly at the two officers in the room. Obviously this was the boss. He looked at us and smiled in a grimacing sort of way, a cigarette clenched between his teeth. I took an instant dislike to

this nasty character and foresaw trouble. He shrieked
again at the man behind the typewriter, who in turn
screamed at his mate, who scuttled off.

After a few minutes the officer returned with a pile of
paper and used carbon copy sheets. All eyes were upon
him as he slowly and meticulously layered up eight
sheets of paper, with a carbon layer between each sheet.
It seemed an enormously thick wad as he aligned it and
fed it into the paper feed. I thought he would never get
anything to copy below the third layer, but I had under-
estimated the force with which he would be hitting the
machine. He began to type, each finger coming down like
a hammer, striking the keys from a distance.

These full-time policemen were so different from the
amiable plump officer and his short mate of the day
before. As he began to type, the keys jammed, a bunch of
them sticking together in a vertical position. After trying
to separate them he spoke to the chief, who shouted
loudly and strode out, obviously angry. I wondered if
this was another show, or a real demonstration of ag-
gression. We had seen some good acting on the previous
day. Such a seemingly genuine manifestation of grief at
our plight had been shown on several occasions, yet on
reflection I could not help but believe it was all a sham.
Now, instead of empathy, outrage was being displayed.

After a few minutes the chief returned with another
typewriter, which he flung on to the desk with such force
that it lifted and moved the table a few inches. For several
seconds he shrieked at his men, before finally composing
himself, clutching his necktie and thrusting his head
forward like a clucking chicken, seemingly calmed by the
ritual. He turned the chair around so that the back was
facing us, straddled it, and folded his arms on the top
rail. I smiled as I recognized this position as a posture
often used in films to re-create scenes of police con-

ducting interviews. Knowing it was all an act did not diminish the ferocity of what was to follow. He stubbed out his cigarette into a plastic cup, lit up another, and turned to face me.

As he was about to speak, I pre-empted him, politely asking, 'Could I have some water and breakfast please?'

He grimaced and said in broken English that I could have the dregs of his coffee, when he had finished it. He picked up the cup, drank the contents and then tapped his cigarette ash into it. With a sarcastic laugh, he passed the cup to me and shrieked, 'Take, take!'

I did not move.

He swung his leg backwards over the seat of the chair, stood up and came towards me, holding out the cup and squeezing it menacingly until it cracked in his fist. I still refused to take it, as his short frame bent over me, cigarette clenched between his teeth, just an inch from my nose. I was overwhelmed by the smell: a mixture of sweat and Camel cigarette smoke mingled with a faint scent of aftershave lotion, despite his unshaven appearance. I could feel the heat of the cigarette as he sucked hard on it, puffing the smoke from the corner of his mouth directly into my face. I did not flinch, determined to hold my ground. He backed away slowly without taking his eyes off me, placed the crumpled cup on the desk, and resumed his position astride the chair with arms on the backrest. I could not help feeling a rush of fear as I felt the other two officers looking intently at me for any reaction.

He looked through our passports, which were on the desk, and began to speak in French.

'I am English,' I stated, 'and do not understand.'

He asked if anyone spoke French. Jacques spoke up. The officer told Jacques that he would have to translate. I said to Jacques that I did not want him to assist. If they needed translation, he should find a proper interpreter. The chief looked angrily at me, obviously understanding what I had said, and then told Jacques to come closer to him. As Jacques stood up, he snapped his fingers telling the officer in the corner to bring in another chair.

The chair was placed between the chief and the bench on which we were sitting. Jacques was now seated with his back to us, between myself and the officer. The inter-rogation began. I could work out most of the questions concerning his age, education, family history, and why he was in Morocco. In fact, they were the same questions posed yesterday. I could not understand why we were going through this all over again.

I did not hear any of Jacques' replies as he was speaking softly and facing the opposite direction, next to the typewriter. He was grilled for more than an hour, while the room filled with cigarette smoke and the type-writer was being furiously hammered with amazing force. It all seemed a theatrical farce. Finally Jacques stood up and Françoise walked towards the chair. She was asked the same questions, responding quietly, until the moment when a confrontation unexpectedly erupted.

Françoise suddenly stood up and shouted to the officer that he had no right to insist that the Bible was a bad book, forbidden in Morocco. I could tell that she was quoting some of Jesus' sayings to him. He sat listening, open-mouthed and dumbfounded while she berated him. He waited until she had stopped, politely thanked her and then told her to return to the bench. I had never thought Françoise capable of such an outburst. She always seemed so subservient with Jacques. I knew very little about her, except for the deep and obvious devotion she had for her husband.

Next it was my turn. The battle was on, and I could feel my heart pounding. He beckoned me over with his finger. I turned to talk with Jacques, pretending I had not seen the gesture. Jacques pointed his elbow in the direction of the officer, urging me to go to him, but I replied quietly that I wanted him to ask me, not beckon with his finger. He must have understood, as he stood up abruptly, and contemptuously shouted at me to stand up and come and sit in the chair. I slowly got up from the hard bench, somewhat relieved to have the opportunity to stretch.

I made my way slowly to the chair, stood behind it, and told him that I would not talk until I was given water. I protested that we had not been provided with anything to eat or drink for over twenty-four hours, and my voice was suffering. For a few seconds, he silently eyed me up and down before pointing to a sink that I had not noticed before, in the corner behind the door.

Slowly, I walked over to it, enjoying the possibility of movement from the hard bench, before I searched for a cup. There wasn't one. I turned on the tap, which gave out a slow trickle of brown-coloured water. As I let it run for a moment, the brown turned to clear water, but I decided it probably wasn't good to drink it anyway. Instead I scooped some into my cupped hand, and wet my lips and face. It was refreshing, if not quenching. Leisurely, I made my way back to the chair, aware of a floating feeling and my inability to move faster, even if I had wanted to. The deprivation of sleep, food and water was taking its toll, and I felt an involuntary tremor pass through my body.

I had already decided on a strategy of refusing to be intimidated, by being difficult or at least uncooperative, unless it was on my own terms. I had no idea if this would work, but firmly believed that we had done nothing wrong, and felt secure and strong in this belief, which seemed to overcome the fear of the moment. I was about to find out if this was practical. As soon as I sat down, he launched into a barrage of questions, shrieking at me in a mixture of French and broken English.

'What's your name? Where did you learn Arabic? Why are you here in Morocco?'

I sat in silence. Until then I did not know they knew that I spoke Arabic.

After half a minute more of questioning, he stopped, looked at me and screeched, 'Answer! Answer!'

I stood up, towering above him and said very quietly, 'If you behave like a decent human being and treat me in a civilised way, I will answer you, but I will not answer anything while you shout and behave like a dog!'

I knew the danger of this statement, although it was not premeditated, and could hear a gasp from the bench behind me. This was a make or break stage in the proceedings. He grabbed my arm roughly, and yanked me towards the window.

Turning to me with his face close to mine, he hissed, 'Do you know that I can take you into the room next door and do anything I want, even kill you, and no one will bother?'

With that he opened the door to the next room and shoved me inside. It was a cell with bars on the window and no furniture.

I looked into his face and smiled. It was an involuntary smile. I did not know what to say but my stubbornness overcame any fear.

He led me back to the chair, and said with quiet contempt, 'Would you please sit down and answer my questions?'

I breathed a great sigh of relief, and said, 'Of course, I would be delighted.'

This battle was won. For the next two hours or more, while I was interrogated, the typewriter pounded deafeningly just a few inches behind my right ear.

The only break in the questioning came about half way through, when we heard a commotion beneath the window. The chief, glancing out, led me across the room to point out a van below, which was being loaded with large bails of marijuana, covered in plastic sheeting.

'This is worth money, you know. Your books are worth nothing to anyone: *nothing!* Do you understand me? They waste my time!' he shrieked.

At that Françoise stood up, came behind me and started to berate him once more, about the worth of the Scriptures. I was amazed, since I did not know that she understood any English. As I listened and tried to pick up a few words of her French, I realized that again he was respectfully listening to her.

When she had finished, he thanked her again for her correction. Relating this incident to a Moroccan friend later, he told me that authorities find it very difficult to deal with women, especially if they begin wailing or screaming. Perhaps he was afraid she would become hysterical. I was astounded and realized that in reality, we had quite a degree of control by refusing to be intimidated. I was still unsure how far we could go. I wondered if he had ever had to deal with people like us before, knowing how terrified most Moroccans are of the police, even those on traffic duty. Indeed, he seemed somewhat taken aback, and it took a few moments for him to compose himself. He lit up another cigarette before continuing.

Next, he brought up the subject of my family history, checking from a paper that must have been compiled the day before. He too could not believe that I did not know the name of my grandfather and father's relatives, and suggested that I was hiding something. There were more questions about my travels, similar to those of the previous day. I did not see the relevance of any of this, but saw no harm in telling him of my extensive travels to most Arab countries. It was a mistake.

I kept returning to my book and to my contacts with the Ministry of Tourism, telling him of my appointment that day. He stopped to telephone the Ministry, and I could hear someone confirming my story. All through the interview the officer behind the typewriter was busy copying from the statement taken the previous day. Only occasionally did the chief interrogator stop firing questions at me and talk with him.

Finally, he was finished with me. Before I got up from the chair, he again came close to my face, and tossing his head towards the bench behind me, he said, 'I like you, you are different from the others.'

As I returned to the bench, I wondered what he was really saying. I concluded that he was referring to the confrontation. Although feeling a wave of satisfaction, I was sure that it would not do me any good.

Another two hours slipped by as Matti and Veikko underwent their interview. This was a laborious affair, since they understood no French and had great difficulty comprehending the chief's English, with his strong accent. At first they insisted on having an interpreter, until they were informed that they would have to wait in the cells, possibly for several weeks for this privilege. Both preferred to accept the struggle of the questioning, in very poor English.

Almost immediately Matti was grilled about his sister's death. Once again, he went into a state of shock, and although wanting to co-operate, could only stutter a few words. The chief derided him for this, but Matti hung his head, unable to muster any response. After several more questions, his ordeal was finally over and Veikko took the chair. Since his understanding of English was poor and he only spoke Finnish, this was a very short affair. That did not stop the typewriter clattering on at a steady pace though.

As I found out later, almost every detail was wrong, apart from our names, which had been copied directly from our passports. This was not surprising, as the officer behind the typewriter did not speak a word of English, and during the entire inquisition only rarely communicated with the chief, who was the only officer who did.

There were occasions when the chief talked with his typist, insisting on certain phrases being written. Although I did not know what they were, I understood that the detailed attention given to the exact phrasing was for legal purposes. The significance of this and its relevance to the case was discovered only long after, when I learned more about the *Procès Verbal*.

Had I known beforehand about this document and how it could be used, I would not have answered a single question without an interpreter being present. Signing the document, not knowing what was written on it and with no lawyer present was absolute madness. However, we were at this stage very naive, and believed what we were told: it was the document required to permit our release.

By now we had been in this room for several hours, and it was late afternoon. I was amazed that the chief had not left the room since he began the questioning, and had not stopped except to light up another cigarette.

Finally the interrogation was over. Even the chief seemed relieved. He looked at us kindly, and told us quite matter-of-factly that we had not committed any offence, and would soon be released. He elaborated that we may have to pay some duty on the books to the customs authorities. I told him that there was no duty on books in Morocco. This fact, I had previously established with bookshops in Tanger, when I had considered publishing my book in Morocco rather than in England. A lawyer had confirmed this at the time. The chief stated that this was now a matter for the customs, not an issue for the police.

The completed forms, heaped on the window-sill, were now separated on the desk and placed into five neat piles, one for each of us. The chief held out his pen towards us in a sweeping movement, indicating that we should come to the desk and sign. I jumped up first, went to the desk and immediately recognized that they looked exactly the same as the documents produced the day before, closely typed very faint Arabic on a form headed in French: *'Proces Verbal'*.

I immediately turned to the others and insisted we should not sign anything unless the police were prepared to translate the documents. They waited for me to elaborate. 'We have no idea what is written on these papers: it could be anything!' I declared. 'Remember yesterday?'

The chief interrupted me as he took Jacques aside and whispered to him in French. Jacques returned and said that the chief had assured him that these were papers for our release: as soon as we had signed, we could return to the yacht. I doubted the truth of this, and asked Jacques what assurance we would be given.

'Weren't we promised exactly the same thing last night?' I protested. 'Look where we ended up!'

Jacques looked at Françoise, and then at me. With tears in his eyes and head bowed, he murmured: 'Have pity on Françoise, she is sick.'

Again, I felt a wave of helplessness pass over me, and considered for a moment. I stated once again that I would not sign mine, but it was up to the others to do what they thought was right. They all signed. I looked at my paper more intently and was certain it was the same as the one we had been told to sign the previous day. I pondered again, then wrote on mine 'not read' in large capital letters, but did not sign it.

The chief collected up the papers and left the room. The two other officers who had been present the whole time – one at the typewriter, the other sitting quietly in a corner – remained for a while. I asked them what was going on. They did not speak any English. Jacques spoke to them in French but they did not seem to understand him either. They shrugged their shoulders, uttered something in Arabic and departed.

We were left alone for some time, and took the opportunity to stand up, stretch, and look out of the window. The van of *hashish* had gone from the yard below. Finally the chief returned and beckoned us to leave. He seemed a different character: quiet and almost friendly.

As we were walking along the corridor, he guided me into a side room, while the others carried on. Inside, seated at a desk was a large elderly lady with peroxide-blonde hair and dressed in a startling, bright-red suit. The chief stayed on in the room while the lady introduced herself as the British Consul from Tanger. She asked the chief politely to leave the room, since we were entitled to meet privately. He told her not to take long and departed. From the friendly exchange, it seemed they knew each other well.

'Well, how have they treated you?' the Consul first asked.

I told her that we had not been beaten or abused.

'They refused us food and water for the past two days. Apart from one glass of orange and a roll twenty-four hours ago. I am feeling very weak and somewhat incoherent.' I told her.

With some fury, she said, 'Really! They should not have treated you like that.'

Then more quietly, she added that it was normal, and she would ensure that we were fed. We never were given a meal or drink while in custody.

'How did you know we were here?' I asked.

'Your wife telephoned this morning from Spain.'

She expressed anger that the police themselves had not informed her.

'They should have called me as soon as you were taken into custody,' she said 'It is their duty to inform the embassy.'

I told her about the interrogation.

She cut me short and snapped, 'You did not sign anything … I hope?'

I affirmed that I had not, but that the others had signed a document in Arabic. Her eyes rolled up to the ceiling, and she then informed me, 'The paper they signed was the *Procès Verbal!* It will be used in evidence at the trial.'

'Trial!' I exclaimed. I was shocked to hear that word. 'But we were told by the chief that we had not committed any offence.'

She re-phrased the sentence by saying, 'You have committed a very grave and stupid offence against the Islamic Kingdom of Morocco, you know.'

I immediately responded that there was no offence in bringing Scriptures into Morocco, as it was indeed an Islamic state, which according to the teachings of Mohammed, respected and upheld the rights of

Christians, even encouraging his followers to read the Bible.

'Look my dear,' she said patronizingly, 'I have lived here in Morocco for many years. You are on your first visit here.'

I realized that it was useless to argue with her, and that she obviously knew much more about our predicament than I did, even if her facts were wrong. Many months of discussion on this subject with her colleagues in Rabat were to follow. I felt too tired to disagree with her.

I complained to her that the police had not allowed us an interpreter, a lawyer, or allowed us to make phone calls.

'The police did not seem to know that I had my mobile phone with me, which is how I was able to contact my wife,' I informed her.

She again huffed and appeared indignant at the withholding of our rights.

Finally she asked if I wanted a lawyer, explaining that she was not allowed to recommend one, but she would leave with me a list of those that the embassy had approved. I pressed her for advice as to which one to choose, but she would only say that there were two in close proximity, both in Tanger. There were none listed in Tetouan.

After twenty minutes or so, she looked at her watch and said, 'I must get back to Tanger. Is there anything further I can do for you – phone a friend or anything?'

I asked her to telephone two friends, one a Moroccan in Tanger, the other an American in Casablanca, to inform them of my situation. She took the numbers and agreed to do so as soon as she got to her office. I thanked her for the visit and did not see her again until several months later.

I was grateful for the visit and did not know what further assistance she could be, especially if she really believed that we had committed a crime.

Later, I was incensed by intense questioning from the British Vice Consul at the Embassy in Rabat, who demanded to know about my friendship with the Moroccan and American national whose phone number I gave to the Consul in Tanger. I also learned later that someone within the embassy had passed on this information and the phone numbers to the Moroccan police, who subsequently questioned me along the same lines about my friends. I was furious at this violation of confidentiality and complained to Vice Consul. This eventually led to an apology from the HM Consul in Rabat.

The only action the embassy took regarding our two days without food and water and the police failure to inform the embassy of our arrest, along with my other complaints, was a formal letter many weeks later to the Justice Ministry, which expressed my dissatisfaction. The response to this was a note stating how well fed we had been in Tetouan Prison (we had never been there!) and that we had been provided with a translator throughout the interrogation process, and given all of our rights. The Consul's response to this was to say that, 'There are some unsatisfactory points of explanation.'

As far as I am aware, this response was never challenged, even though the Consul and the Ambassador knew it was false, suggesting in writing that I would, 'find this answer objectionable'.

After the British Consul departed I went in search of my friends, who were to be found under the supervision of a jovial fellow who spoke English. I asked him what was happening, and he said we would shortly be going to the court-house. I was again shaken and asked him what the charges were. He told us not to worry, as it was only a very minor offence.

I was anxious, as the ground seemed to constantly shift beneath our feet, always taking us in a more precarious direction. The police chief interrogator arrived and thanked us politely for our co-operation and left us with another officer, who led us to the stairwell. We began to descend. My mind was racing again. This was like a yo-yo. One minute we were buoyed up with hope of release, the next we were on the way to court. Worse still, we could be returning to the dungeon, for all I knew.

This was all so unreal. All those around us were like actors: the feigned sadness of the police the previous night, as we descended these stairs to the cells; the fearsome anger of the chief today, until after the interview, when he transformed into a quiet-spoken, consoling friend; the indignant expression on the face of the Consul, herself a caricature, as I told her of our treatment. Could it all be just a bad dream, I kept wondering?

7. Return to the Dungeon

Monday 1st June 5pm

As we descended the stairs I began to thank God once more that I had been able to contact Spain to alert friends about our situation. I was still not certain if we were under arrest. The police continued to insist that we were not, but I felt sure that it was incompetence on their part that allowed me to keep the phone, albeit concealed, rather than any indication that we were not being held under arrest. Who knows how long we would have been in this position, if I had not been able to contact the outside world?

I kept silent as we were led into the now familiar basement beneath the building. We entered through the sliding steel doors. Once again we went through the ritual of taking everything out of our pockets and then had to remove our belts and shoelaces before being frisked down. Everything seemed to be moving at a faster rate now.

We were quickly led through the gate and down towards the cell at the end of the passageway, the same one from which I had seen a black face peering through the grille on the previous night. Again, Françoise was separated from us, as we heard shouting and banging coming from inside the cell. When the door was opened, everything went silent. I peered into the gloom, and could make out several pairs of large white eyes staring at us from the floor, but little else. This cell was much larger, and even had its own very dim lamp in the ceiling.

To our left as we entered was a low wall partitioning off the area of floor where the hole was contained. A trickle of water was noisily running down the wall into the hole, and someone was squatting over it. The cell was thick with the smell emanating from this hole, mixed with body odour. There was another smell that I recognized: marijuana. This cell was much warmer than the previous one and the floor was almost completely carpeted with those same brown, woollen blankets, although much dirtier and more matted than the ones we wrapped around ourselves in the other cell.

As the door slammed loudly behind us it did not take long to adjust to the dim light. I could make out that most of the floor was taken up with dark brown, shining, almost naked bodies, lying full length, with heads propped against the wall, feet towards the centre of the room. The bodies and blankets seemed to merge. A few inmates stood up briefly and then sank back into their places, spread around the wall. We looked for a place to sit or lie down but there seemed to be no room, apart from in the centre, at their feet. At first, no one seemed willing to make room for us and the atmosphere seemed hostile.

We stood for a few minutes, feeling out of place, aware that all eyes were fixed on us. I had no previous experience like this and could find nothing in my memory to provide clues as to how to react or behave in the circumstances. I again thought of films I had seen and began to worry about the possibility of being attacked.

Thinking more rationally, I then greeted them in Arabic, *'Salam Alikhum'* and placed my right hand across my heart in the traditional way.

Thankfully, I received the same hearty response from everyone in the cell and could see white teeth grinning towards me. It was a great relief.

Jacques then spoke to them in French. He was able to converse with several inmates, most of whom, it transpired, were from Central Africa. Much of the conversation was full of jovial greetings and general questions on how long they had been there. Soon they sat up and made a space for him. Several others then began to shuffle around, making room by sitting up against the wall. They then invited me to recline with them.

I began to converse in a mixture of Arabic and Spanish and discovered that my nearest neighbour was Algerian.

'Where have you all come from?' I asked, thinking they were all here for the same reason.

Pointing to the others, he said: 'These are illegal immigrants from Senegal, Sierra Leone, Mauritania, one from Nigeria and others from further south in Africa. I'm Algerian.'

I asked him how they had travelled so far north.

'They walked!' he laughed, astonished at the absurd question.

I began to realize the lengths to which people would go to escape poverty, persecution or just to seek a better life. Some must have walked for literally thousands of miles. I felt real admiration for them.

'What will be their fate?' I enquired.

They would be returned by ship from Casablanca, when one was found to be going south.

'How would this get you home to Algeria?'

'I'm not going anywhere,' he stated bluntly, but did not elaborate. I presumed he was in for deeper trouble than merely immigration offences, and did not pry further.

There were nineteen men in the cell, and most had been here for over two weeks, awaiting trial. Once again, a wave of fear and a sweat rolled over me, as I contemplated the thought of having to stay here for that length of time. It was highly possible.

'Have you been fed?' I asked.

He laughed loudly and shouted my question to the others in French.

They all laughed as he explained to me, 'The guard brings in a plastic bucket, once a day. It contains a liquid with peelings in it.'

I added: *'Wa Lahma Kaman?'* (and meat too).

He chuckled, obviously realizing I was referring to the live maggots I saw on the top of the peelings in the bucket so many hours ago.

No one spoke any English, so I continued to struggle on in Arabic, although it was not the first language of most there. Apart from the Algerian next to me, there was one other Algerian and a Moroccan. These North Africans did not seem as friendly and gregarious as the Central Africans, but at least I could communicate with them.

As in our previous cell there was no furniture: absolutely nothing except the blankets. These were rolled up at the walls to form a long continuous pillow. Others were laid out like carpets to cover the bare concrete floor nearer the centre. Somehow, with all those people packed together, this cell was actually quite warm and cosy: even comfortable and inviting in comparison with our previous one, despite the smell. Having so many friendly people around was stimulating and a blessing. Even if not a step nearer freedom, it was a big step nearer humanity and I soon felt comfortable there.

Veikko and Matti, who were silent, lay curled up near the centre by our feet on the only space left on the floor. I talked with Matti for some time and tried to reassure him. I wished I could offer physical reassurance by placing my arm around him, but did not dare to do so, for fear of being misinterpreted by those around us. He was concerned for Veikko, who had a heart condition and needed medication on a daily basis. Several times, he had made this clear to the guards, but they had ignored it. 'What could be done?' he asked.

It was useless to press for anything, even water, as we had discovered. I was surprised that Veikko was not taking a stronger moral lead with Matti. Although I did not know either of them well, I had gathered that Veikko was someone Matti looked up to, possibly his pastor or at least a father figure. Yet he seemed to have retreated into a shell. Perhaps the strain of the situation was just too much for him to handle.

Jacques discovered that one of the Africans who spoke French was a fellow Christian, so they enjoyed together a deep and happy time of true fellowship. Just as we were getting used to our surroundings, the guard returned noisily and opened the door. Several people stood up expectantly. Standing in the doorway he shouted out some names. No one responded. He tried again with different pronunciations of what sounded like Zulu names. One fellow still reclining, stood up and walked over to the guard. Handcuffs were snapped on his wrists, while the guard continued the roll call. With no further response, he took the man, slammed the door, and locked it.

We returned to our places and shuffled around to make room for Matti and Veikko against the wall. Shortly afterwards the guard returned, this time with a longer list of names. Almost everyone stood up this time and walked towards the door. Again, the guard checked his list before ten of them were handcuffed together in a line and led away.

We were left with plenty of room now and immediately started to re-organize the blankets. I began to unroll one that had been used as a pillow, and was surprised to see cigarette butts fall out. A closer look revealed that they were marijuana joints. There were dozens of them under the other rolled blankets. I swept them back underneath, re-rolled the 'pillow', and shook out the other blankets. They were filthy: grit and dust flew out of them. I wondered if it was better to leave the dirt undisturbed. The other inmates watched, but did not assist.

I made myself comfortable and tried to sleep, but without success. There was too much to take in and think about. The still air of the unventilated cell smelled thick and musty and I regretted my attempts at cleaning it. In fact, I felt stupid and embarrassed at having tried to. The body odour and stench from the toilet hole was still overpowering. With only a few of us left, the room now felt very spacious and different. The jailer soon returned to throw back one of the men previously taken away. As he fell to the floor, it became obvious that he had been beaten, although he did not look badly hurt. We helped him to the blankets and another prisoner spoke comforting words to him, stroking his face.

Settling back, I began to meditate on the day's experiences, purposefully trying to memorize everything: the interrogations, my feelings and moments of terror, the smells and sights that surrounded me, the shape of the cell, the number and nationalities of each person there and some of their names. From early childhood I had learned to do this.

At the age of four my parents had separated and my two-year-old brother and I were placed in a children's home. Once there, I began hiding away at every opportunity, retreating into my own very private world consisting only of memories. I knew instinctively that I would survive only if what I could recall was kept alive, and not allowed to slip away. I would recollect every event, from the time I could first remember, until I was taken into care and separated from my parents.

I would skulk off for hours as a child, to think back and reflect on each minute detail of our flat in Pangbourne: the smells, the sound of trains thundering past, colours, each item of furniture and the pictures on the walls. Details of the sights and events I witnessed from our window overlooking the road were especially significant. Why these memories were so important I never really understood. I was always looking for continuity and reason in the past for my present circumstances, which seemed so desolate, never able to comprehend why I had been abandoned, especially to this home which I hated. For years I waited expectantly for my mother to come and collect me.

How ironic that I was now in a similar situation at over fifty years old: taken to a strange place and mentally recording everything I could, in case the memories slipped away, again awaiting rescue.

8. Meeting the King's Prosecutor

Monday 1st June 7pm

After several hours the guard returned and this time called our names. We were to meet the King's Prosecutor. The British Consul had informed me during her visit earlier in the day that he was the one to decide if we would be charged or not.

We were led back through the corridor and as we passed the cell doors I looked through each grille for signs of life. Nothing, except for a woman in the second cell, her knuckles clutching the bars. All I could see of her face was a fawn headscarf draped over her hair, while her other hand gripped one end across her mouth. Only her nose and her penetrating wide eyes were visible.

Françoise was waiting in the larger basement room, having been released ahead of us. Once again our possessions were returned; we replaced our belts and shoelaces and were escorted to the door. It was a surprise that I did not feel any weaker than the previous time: we still had not been given a meal or water. Perhaps the repetition of the routine had taken some of the fear and foreboding out of our situation, and had released the stress I previously felt.

We were led through the iron doors into the courtyard where two other prisoners were waiting. Our warder gestured for us to wait, while a battered white Citroën van reversed in front of us. One prisoner in handcuffs was pushed roughly into the back of it leaving him sprawled on the floor. An officer jumped in after him, slamming the door and the van roared off. Another similar van reversed, and the rear doors were opened to reveal a narrow wooden plank lining each side. We were politely signalled to enter. It was a relief that handcuffs were not put on us.

Two officers sat in the front, while another closed the rear doors, and we drove off. With nothing to hold onto, or to brace against, it was difficult not to slip off the seat as we went up the ramp and swung through the streets. It was evening, and we could feel the heat and humidity radiating inside the van. It felt good to be back at ground level with the dungeon receding behind us.

We reached an open square in the centre of Tetouan where the van stopped. The rear doors were opened and a rush of cooler air enveloped us. Many people crowded around to peer in as we emerged. It felt wonderful to be out into the open air again, where the low evening sunlight was turning the sky pink.

The fruit market was nearby and although closed now, the smells of overripe fruit wafted across the square. I recognized this area, having stopped at several of the nearby cafés during shopping trips, seeking relief from the heat after a few hours of exhausting bartering in the *souk*, the local market. The bazaar was diagonally opposite, less than a hundred metres away. The refreshing smell of mint tea was also in the air wafting from a nearby café.

Taking stock of our surroundings, I noticed the ancient palms swaying above our heads. The sparrows in the

Typical Berber market in M'Diq.

trees chirped away, as they always did at this time of the evening, while they covered the paving slabs below with their small white droppings. Although I knew exactly where we were, I did not recognize the entrance of the imposing elevated, colonial-style building up several steps behind us.

The beautiful, Moroccan-style arched door was guarded by armed police officers. Obviously this was the court-house. The van that had preceded us drew alongside, and three prisoners chained together emerged. The first was the same man we had witnessed being loaded in at the interrogation centre. Where had they collected the other two? I assumed that it was from the local prison.

Gaunt, unshaven and with their heads bowed, they were a miserable sight as they staggered and were pushed past the van towards the steps. I wondered what they had been through and why. They were marshalled up the steps towards the guarded door – confirmation that we were indeed at the court-house. All eyes from the crowd followed them, as one of our policemen ushered us from behind and through the doorway. It was a strange time to feel embarrassed by inquisitive looks, but I was glad to reach the other side of the door, away from those staring eyes.

Once inside, we found ourselves in an enclosed courtyard filled with people crowding and jostling. Looking up, I noticed a huge glass roof crowning three floors, with tiered galleries. These were also crowded with people peering down. From the centre hung an enormous chandelier, which reached down to the level of the first floor. Natural light streamed down into the centre. The wooden-framed galleries were decorated with brightly coloured ceramic tiles set into patterns known as *zillij*. As the policeman led us to the stairs I admired the grandeur of this typical nineteenth-century Islamic design. It was magnificent. As we wound our way up to the second floor, it became less crowded and I could now see the building was most probably a palace originally – that of the town mayor or *Muktar*.

We were taken to a large room with rows of benches, and led to one near the back. I began to panic. If this was the court and we were to be tried immediately, where was our lawyer, embassy representative and interpreter? I asked the policeman for a drink. He called to one of the men nearby, who scuttled off. Some minutes later he returned with a large bottle of water. I offered it to Françoise, who took a few sips. Our police officer left, and we seemed to be alone, apart from a small group of people sitting on a bench close to the front of the court.

We sat down and shared the water between us. Despite intense thirst, it was not easy to drink. The action of tilting my head back seemed to create a gagging sensation that made me want to choke. We each took small sips and passed it around, until the bottle was empty. A fellow in a shabby blue tracksuit came into the room, and I asked him if he could get us more water. He took our empty bottle and disappeared. I tried to follow him to see where he got it from, but he was too quick.

We had no idea what was happening. I pulled out my mobile phone and turned it on. To my delight, there was a signal and still some life in the battery. I asked my friends to surround me, as I made a call to Anne in Spain. I was concerned that it may be forbidden and that the phone would be taken away. I dialled and got a ringing tone. As Anne answered, I felt transported.

Suddenly it was as if I was no longer in Morocco, but actually at home. She asked what was happening but without expressing concern in her voice. After all, she had no idea about our treatment, even though I had informed her of our detention in my brief report earlier in the day. At that point, I had no idea just how much trouble we were in.

Our circumstances seemed so bizarre and unexpected. Once again I took a deep breath and wondered if this was all a dream. After all, I felt rather strange and seemed to be floating again. Anne then explained that she had received a call from the British Consul, who told her that we had been arrested and could face serious charges. This was quite worrying to hear and brought me back to reality.

I told her that we had not been allowed a translator, food, water, or access to a lawyer, but that we were now sitting in a courtroom and did not know what would transpire next. There did not seem much else to say, except to ask her to inform as many of our friends as possible about the situation. I reluctantly disconnected and savoured the last seconds of home in Spain, wondering when I would be there again, before mentally returning to my surroundings. I informed the others of our conversation, although they had heard everything. The fellow returned with the bottle refilled. I wondered again where he had obtained it, but it did not really matter; I was going to drink it anyway.

We waited there for an hour or more without any supervision. Then a group of lawyers entered, dressed in black cloaks and white tuckers. I presumed they were attending on our behalf. I noticed how similar this archaic dress was to that of the clergy. As they came towards us, I noticed that there was a large man with them who seemed to be the centre of attention. He was dressed in a white robe with a black jacket. His head was bowed and he looked familiar.

It was the fat man from the jail. I looked down at his feet just to make sure: yes, there were those sandals, it was definitely him. The group stood very close to us in the side aisle, talking in hushed tones. Suddenly they scurried off, leaving the large man alone with a short, wiry fellow wearing baggy trousers. They sat down together in front of us, looking very solemn. After some time they got up and the fat man walked out. His wiry friend came over to us and, apparently guessing our concerns, told us not to worry; all would be OK. I asked him what he could tell us, as it seemed that he knew more than we did.

The man spoke good English and said this was the court where the King's Prosecutor oversaw proceedings.

'You will be given the opportunity to speak with him: he will decide your fate. He is a good man!' he said.

'Why are we here? What are the charges? What will happen to us?' I asked.

He would not or could not elaborate, although we did press him for more information.

'Don't worry,' he said, 'this is a simple matter. You have done nothing wrong.'

'Can you get us any food and water?' I enquired.

'Do you have any money?' he asked.

I pulled out a 50 Dirham note and gave it to him. Off he went, returning half an hour later with five rolls wrapped in greaseproof paper, but no water. He was very talkative and told us he was a policeman, working in the town.

It had been a long time since food had passed our lips. I savoured every small bite of this *shroumer* – a long roll containing spiced meat and lettuce. We pumped the man for more information, and he explained the duties of the King's Prosecutor. It seemed that he acted as an intermediary between the Crown Prosecution and the Defence. It was his responsibility to decide whether a case should come to trial. I was optimistic that he would see the stupidity of our detention.

I asked the officer about the other people who were waiting near the front of the court. They were all there on drugs charges, mostly for attempting to export marijuana to Spain. They would be fined 100 or 200 Dirhams and set free. If they could not pay, they would be imprisoned for a few months, depending on how many kilos had been in their possession when they were caught.

After sitting in the courtroom for several hours, we were called to the upper level. The corridor was empty, and we could see over the balcony into the courtyard below, where a tall palm tree was standing. We were told to wait outside the door by the wooden rail of the balcony, on which we leaned. Finally the door opened and a man invited us inside. The room was small, most of it filled by a large mahogany desk, behind which sat a handsome man dressed in an immaculate suit which fitted him perfectly. At last we were face to face with the King's Prosecutor. I had never seen such a well-dressed

Moroccan in my life. He was absorbed in chatting and laughing to someone on the other end of his mobile phone.

Now I was really optimistic. Here was an intelligent-looking man, with whom we could discuss our situation. He pressed the button to terminate his call. The telephone on his desk rang noisily. He picked it up and straightened his back as he spoke in very sincere, deep tones. All the while, he was eyeing us closely. I deliberately looked him in the eye to calculate if he was prepared for eye contact. He was, but only briefly. He put down the phone and began to speak in French.

After a few sentences, he noticed vacant expressions on our faces. He looked at Veikko, Matti and me, rather than at Jacques, who was on the other side of the desk. In French he asked if we understood. I told him that we did not speak French, but that Jacques did. He then conversed a little with Jacques, who looked at me but could not translate what was being said. He turned up his hands in frustration, shrugging his shoulders. The councillor spoke to the other Moroccan in the room and asked him to take us out. This man spoke English and explained that he needed an interpreter. Not wishing any delay in getting our situation resolved, I told him that his English was fine.

'No' he said, 'we need a proper interpreter.'

I was somewhat relieved. At last we were going to find out what was going on from someone who obviously had real authority.

Once again we were told to wait outside the prosecutor's office, so we chatted amongst ourselves while leaning on the balcony rail looking over to the central courtyard below. It was well over an hour before the officer returned with another man. After knocking on the door they went straight into the office, and closed the door behind them. We could hear soft voices inside. It sounded serious.

At last the door opened and we were ushered inside. We took up our positions as before, with Jacques and Françoise on one side of the desk and Matti, Veikko and myself on the other. The officer and the interpreter stood behind the King's Prosecutor.

Looking at me, with the new man translating, he asked in French, 'What are you doing here?'

'My friends and I came with my yacht. I am working on a book in co-operation with the Ministry of Tourism. It is a nautical pilot for North Africa.'

He peered down at some papers with a puzzled look on his face.

I continued, 'I have been working on it for several years, and have never had any problems here before.'

He looked up and said, 'No, this is your first visit to Morocco, for all of you!'

I protested with a forced laugh and said, 'No, Sir, I have been visiting for over thirty years, and have travelled in at least ten times over the past year alone, and Jacques,' I told him, 'lives here in Morocco.'

He then asked, 'Why did you come here illegally?'

'What do you mean illegally?' I asked.

The interpreter said, 'Why did you not get your passports stamped? How did you enter Morocco?'

I laughed again, and said, 'Take a look,' pointing to the passports on his desk. 'We all entered in the normal way, and there is a stamp in all our passports to prove it.'

Strangely, he did not open the passports. I wondered where he got his information, and then noted that the paper he was looking at was the same document we had been asked to sign: the *Procès Verbal*. Which version was it, I wondered? The Sunday or the Monday edition?

He leaned back in his chair and asked, 'What about the books? To whom were you going to give them?'

In an instant I decided to speak on behalf of Matti, although he was the one caught with the books. 'We were bringing them for Jacques,' I replied and added, 'I often bring books to Morocco to give as presents to people who ask for them.'

He responded, 'But you can buy these in Morocco.'

I decided not to challenge this statement. 'Yes' I said.

I explained that it was a Moroccan custom always to bring a present whenever visiting a friend or relative, and that I had made many friends. It was normal to bring a Bible, as many Moroccans had given me a Qur'an as a gift. Jacques was our friend, I explained, and he also had made friends who asked for Bibles.

He asked again 'Why did you enter illegally and why did you not clear customs on entry?'

'Sir' I said, 'I cleared customs in the normal way. Captains are required to sign a form stating they do not have firearms, ammunition, excess spirits or tobacco on board, and I signed this declaration. I have a copy of it on the yacht.' I also informed him that a customs officer had boarded the yacht with a police officer on our arrival. They had seen my books, which were in the main cabin.

He asked, 'You cleared customs in the marina?'

'Yes,' I confirmed. He again looked puzzled, but seemed content with this response as he rocked back in his chair.

I now realized that the *Procès Verbal* must have falsely stated that we had entered illegally as well as having failed to clear customs: something quite impossible in any port in Morocco. I wondered what other false information was contained in that document. It would be several weeks, long after the trial, before I really discovered the contents.

After thinking for a while, he smiled and then nodded, and as he picked up the papers, he told us that we had been naive.

'This is a Muslim country and the Bible is a difficult book for some people to understand,' he declared through the interpreter. 'However you have not committed any crime against the law, only a minor customs offence. You should have filled out a different form.'

I understood the French word for 'indiscretion'. I had heard that before.

'You will pay a small fine to the customs and return to your boat tonight. This has nothing to do with the court and is not a police matter.' He reiterated: 'It is a minor indiscretion.'

I asked him how much we would have to pay.

'Only a nominal amount,' he assured me.

I pressed further for a figure, and was told: approximately 100 Dirhams ($10). I was happy to pay this and thanked him; assuring him that I would be glad to pay whatever small fee the customs required. He did not respond, and was quickly back on his mobile phone, cheerily talking to someone as we were ushered out of the room by the two officers.

A great feeling of relief came over me as the interpreter closed the door.

'What's the procedure now?' I asked. He said we would go down and pay some money to the customs: an officer was always on duty in the court, he assured me. I again asked how much and he affirmed, 'probably around 100 Dirhams'.

At this stage, I would have been pleased to pay anything, if it meant going home. I had 500 Dirhams in cash, which would be sufficient. One of the officers told us he would go to find the customs official, who should be somewhere nearby.

Returning to another courtroom, on the same upper level as the office we had just left, we waited. This room was identical to the one below, although a little smarter. It was now past midnight; no one else was around apart from some police on the ground floor guarding the entrance, but the King's Prosecutor was still working. We could hear him in the office chatting on the phone.

A few minutes later the officer who spoke English, but who did not interpret, returned. He said he could not find the duty customs officer and therefore he needed to see the King's Prosecutor again. We followed him to the office but he held his hands up to indicate that we should wait outside as he entered.

After a few minutes, he emerged to tell us, 'You will have to return to the cells.'

'What? If we have not committed any crime, why should we have to return to the cells?' I argued.

'Because the duty customs officer is not in the building: he has gone home.'

I protested that this was not our fault and suggested that instead, perhaps we could pay money now: even as much as 1,000 Dirhams ($100) to be released.

I pointed to Françoise, 'She is ill and we do not want to go back to the cells,' I told him.

The others were silent as the conversation continued. Knocking lightly, he re-entered the prosecutor's office and we tried to hear their discussion.

After a few minutes they both emerged, and the King's Prosecutor said through the policeman, 'You need to deposit 10,000 Dirhams until you return to the court on Wednesday. Then you will pay a small fine to the customs, and the rest of the money will be refunded. The trial will be on Wednesday.'

'Trial? But Sir, you said we had not committed any offence against the law!' I exclaimed.

In perfect English, he replied, 'There will be a trial and you will have to return on Wednesday.'

Again, I protested that we would pay anything not to return to the cells.

As they walked down the passageway, the two men discussed the matter further. They stopped, turned and asked if we had 10,000 Dirhams.

'We could get it,' I said as I pulled out my visa card. We could draw it from a cash machine. There was more talk between the two of them, and then the policeman said there were no machines in Tetouan.

'There are several, and I know exactly where they are,' I told him with far more confidence than I felt.

I knew of at least one, although I could not remember where it was. I had no intention of returning to the cells.

After a few parting words, the prosecutor strode off and the policeman said, 'OK, we will go to the machine. Then you can go home.'

We hastened down the stairs and into the street, past the guard on the door and into the cool night air. A surprising number of people were milling around the square.

'Where is the ATM machine?' the officer asked.

I had to admit that I was not exactly sure. The officer went up to a passer-by in the street and asked if he knew of one. He pointed in the direction of the main street.

By now, I was orientated and realized that this was indeed where a machine was located, near to the market. Perhaps it would not accept my credit card, or maybe it would not dispense enough cash. On arrival, I immediately saw that it did not list visa amongst the cards advertised.

'There must be another machine,' I told the officer.

There was another bank further along towards the fruit market, I recalled. We continued down the street and finally, in the distance, we saw the other bank. This was the one.

It was a great relief to observe the familiar visa sign above the machine. Several people were leaning against the wall nearby, but they moved away as we closed in. I placed my card in the slot, and typed in my pin number, hoping I remembered it correctly. The screen told me to wait, then asked how much cash I wanted. To my surprise it listed up to 4,000 Dirhams. We needed another 6,000 Dirhams. I typed in the maximum and waited.

Sometimes these machines do not give out the maximum amount requested, and then they reject further attempts. The machine clattered inside before returning my card. After a few anxious seconds, the cash was dispensed. I counted the notes. Now Matti admitted that he also had his card and moved in to get another 4,000 Dirhams. I used a second card for the final transaction. With this 4,000 Dirhams we would also have cash for the taxi back to the yacht. To our great relief, the machine chattered away and finally ejected this too. We had the money and would not have to spend another night in the cells. I felt elated.

As we walked back towards the court, I asked the policeman why the King's Prosecutor had changed his mind from one minute to the next. He did not answer. I pressed him further and finally he said we should not worry, it was just a formality, for the sake of the customs authorities.

When we arrived back at the court, the policeman told us to wait on the ground floor, while he found the official who would take the money. I wondered who could possibly be around at this time of morning; it was now well after midnight. Determined not to return to the cells, I began to think of contingency plans, even the possibility of running off into the street, if it came to that. After all, there were no guards within sight.

While we waited, the King's Prosecutor came down the stairs. As he passed and looked in our direction, I questioned him politely.

'Sir, why are we being charged?'

'Be in court on Wednesday and all will be well.'

I asked about my friends and he said, 'No. Just you.'

A sleepy-looking old man dressed in a long, brown Moroccan caftan came shuffling noisily down the stairs. He wore the traditional heel-less, bright yellow pointed slippers with curling toes. I wondered how on earth he kept them on his feet, as he descended the stairs. He unlocked a door nearby, entered and switched on the light, revealing this to be the accounting office. He opened a huge ledger, which immediately brought back frightening memories from the jail, and sat down to write in it. It took half an hour before he had completed the entry, and another ten minutes to slowly count the cash twice or maybe three times. Finally, he wrote out a receipt and handed it to me, stowing away the cash in the safe behind his desk. It was now well past two o'clock. At last, we were free to leave.

The policeman then informed us that we had to obtain the signature of the King's Prosecutor before we could go. I was amazed that he was still here; I had assumed his descent down the stairs meant that he was on his way home. We returned to his office, and were immediately ushered in to wait by his desk as he filled in five orange forms, one for each of us.

He handed them to us, and mentioned again, 'Be sure to return on Wednesday, or you will be in trouble.'

We agreed, but I was confused, 'Who exactly needs to be there?' I asked again.

'All of you. You will all be charged in court.' I could not understand why he kept changing his mind, but did not press him further. I never did figure it out.

As soon as we reached the steps leading down to the square, we hugged each other and set off in search of a taxi to take us to the marina, twenty kilometres away. On the way we talked about finding a restaurant, but realized that nothing would be open. We soon found a taxi and jumped in. It was a huge relief to be leaving the court behind us.

Feeling a mixture of elation and weariness, we spoke little on the journey. It seemed we were all equally stunned and bewildered by the events of the last two days. As we rounded the final corner into the still empty marina, we saw the yacht. I noticed an open café, and after an argument with the driver, who wanted more than double the usual price, we discussed whether we should eat.

Jacques and Françoise decided to return to their nearby apartment, while the rest of us chose to eat. It would be impossible to sleep without some food inside us when we were this hyped up, or so we thought. We knew it was a big mistake as soon as the meal was served up. It consisted of reheated dry chicken and chips with nothing fresh. It was not at all appetizing, despite the deprivations we had experienced. I ate very little, but drank a large bottle of water. We did not want to discuss our incarceration.

Finally we paid for the meal and returned to the yacht. What a wonderful feeling it was to step on board: feeling the movement under my feet, breathing in the smell of the sea and realizing our ordeal was over: at least for tonight.

Once again it felt like stepping off a roller coaster, a feeling that was becoming all too familiar.

9. Awaiting Trial

Tuesday 2nd June 6am

I awoke feeling very thirsty and aching all over, not knowing at first quite where I was. There was silence in the port, although it was daylight. I had only slept for two hours, so I turned over and tried to return to sleep. It was difficult, as the realization of the past two days filled my mind. I felt cramp in my feet, due to dehydration and lack of salt, so I drank half a bottle of water and finally managed to doze off again.

It was the sound of feet on the deck that woke me. They were soft, short steps, so I knew that Veikko was up. He was an elderly, retired man who had been a fisherman all his life, according to Matti who liked to boast of his friend's skills as a ship's captain. He had displayed no interest in assisting with the yacht or in fishing when I offered him the tackle on the trip over. I assumed that this was because of his age, and did not press him. From his rugged features I guessed that he must be in his seventies, although it was difficult to tell.

Matti had told me of their adopted country, and of Veikko's hometown, Ladysmith, on Vancouver Island, a logging and fishing town where there was a large Finnish population who had settled there years ago. Apparently most of the inhabitants spoke neither English nor French, but retained their Finnish language and culture. I found it very difficult to understand anything Veikko said.

He looked every inch a fisherman, with his short, muscular, rugged frame and deeply etched face. He always woke early and went for a walk. In fact I began to resent his strange mannerisms. Hands clasped behind his back, peaked cap pulled down hard, head bowed and shoulders hunched, he would walk looking from side to side over each shoulder in turn, as if he were being followed. He could not help it and had probably done it all his life, but it still annoyed me. I began to wonder how I had come to be in all this trouble with these two guys who I did not even know or understand.

Our association had begun in Malaga, Spain, where I had been invited to attend a conference for individuals, including businessmen, interested in North Africa. One of my main interests in attending had been my book project, which I had been working on for years while sailing in the Maghreb. Covering each port over two thousand miles of coastline in the Mediterranean and on the Atlantic coast of Morocco, I was anxious to gain more knowledge of the country. I received help from the Moroccan and Tunisian governments and was given a letter of introduction and authorization from the Moroccan Minister of the Interior, following several meetings with officials.

One Canadian friend at the conference told me of a very wealthy colleague (it turned out to be Matti) who had just sold a business in Canada and who wanted to invest in Morocco. He had visited the country the previous year but had such a terrible experience there that he abandoned his plan, wanting nothing more to do with the country.

Asking what had happened I was told how he had gone with a friend to Tanger, intending to stay several days to explore the country and its opportunities. From the beginning, he was harassed by young 'tour guides' who would not leave him alone. When he rejected their offers he was crowded by a group of youths who tried to put their hands in his pockets. One youth cursed him in Finnish. He was so angry by the end of the first day that he decided to return to Spain, vowing never to return.

His ordeal was not yet over. While waiting in the customs hall of the port, a customs officer approached him and asked what was in a bag he was carrying.

'Clothes,' he told them. They looked inside and found only clothes and his razor.

He was escorted to a room, where money was demanded. He was livid and began shouting at them. They forcibly strip-searched him, ostensibly looking for drugs. He had never even smoked cigarettes in his life, and was shaking with anger by the time he emerged. I knew all this was plausible, because even though all of my four children were familiar with Morocco, the same experience had happened to one of my daughters – Sera – on a visit to Tanger with her husband. She has never returned there since.

My friend half jokingly challenged me to take Matti to Morocco on my yacht, to show him what the people were really like and, hopefully, to change his mind about investing there. It was a challenge I could not resist. We subsequently corresponded and I assured him that Tanger was not representative of the real Morocco. He had only two requests: to bring his fisherman friend along, and to gain my permission to bring a few Bibles for the French Christian couple whom I had told him about.

As I slowly climbed out of my bunk in the rear cabin of the yacht, it was difficult to comprehend or believe what we had been through during the past two days. I met Matti in the lounge. He looked haggard and his short, fair hair was in a mess, but he said that he had slept well. We went to the upper deck and noticed that we were still the only yacht in the harbour. It was a very peaceful morning with the usual police strolling around. The deck was still wet with dew, and I wiped the seats down before we sat in the cockpit. I waited for Matti to begin a conversation, but he said little. I was happy to stay in my shell too.

Usually there were at least a dozen people to be seen wandering around the port during the day. On previous visits I had assumed that they lived there, but soon realized after seeing the same men pacing up and down every day, that they were all plain-clothed police officers on their shift. I later learned that virtually nobody actually lived in the port, except during the month of August, when many wealthy Moroccans from Casablanca and Rabat spent their vacation in the apartments of the port.

We sat on deck and waited for Veikko to return before making plans for the day. We were still shocked and quite dazed. I tried to piece together our position in relation to the police and the court, still unsure if we were in trouble or not. It seemed logical that since the police were involved, there would be formalities to go through before we could be cleared to depart. I called Anne and gave her an update. She sounded very worried, and told me that she had passed the information to friends in Spain, as I had requested. I warned her that publicity may be a problem, but I really did not know.

My greatest difficulty was only beginning: one minute I was elated by good news or a hopeful conversation, only to be plunged into deep despair the next.

We saw Veikko walking back to the yacht, looking nervously from side to side. I mentioned to Matti how suspicious he looked. He laughed and nodded: the first time I had seen him smile in days. We decided to visit

Jacques in his apartment and talk things through with him. One of the plain-clothed officers followed us at a discreet distance. I turned and waved at him as Jacques opened the door and he turned away, looking embarrassed. We were warmly welcomed and joined him and Françoise for coffee. I wondered about the wisdom of visiting, but could see no harm in it. We talked for more than an hour, though with great difficulty, as Jacques seemed even less able to communicate than before. We did agree to make it a priority to contact a lawyer, for Jacques to call his French Embassy, and for Veikko and Matti to approach their Canadian Ambassador or Consul.

We were very tired but only had one day in which to prepare for the trial. I had my laptop computer on board and could connect it to my mobile phone, so was able to continue to write and receive e-mails. This was to become instrumental over the coming months, as I stayed in touch with the outside world in a way not technically possible even two years before.

We were just within phone coverage of Ceuta, which is under Spanish government control. With an extra aerial connected to the phone to increase signal strength, I could use the Spanish mobile phone network, where my phone was billed, rather than using the Moroccan system. In this way, telephone calls were far cheaper and more secure. I set about making up the antenna to connect to the phone, using skills learned during my time as an electronics engineer in the Royal Navy. By calculating the wavelength and constructing a short stub antenna to the mast of the yacht, and then running a cable down to the back cabin, I soon had a good signal and the phone connected to my computer.

I began writing my first e-mail, informing influential friends throughout the world of our predicament. I was in business. Most of that day was spent on my computer, writing a detailed diary and log of the past few days, including notes of all the conversations. At this point I told friends not to make anything public in case it annoyed the authorities.

From the list of lawyers given to me by the British Consul, I selected the nearest one in Tanger, and called him. He spoke reasonable English and excellent Spanish. After I had informed him of the nature of the case, he said he would get more information from the court. It was now Tuesday, less than a day away from the hearing. The lawyer said he would arrange a postponement until Friday, giving him time to prepare. I asked when he wanted to meet with me.

'Oh, let's meet half an hour before the trial. That should give us sufficient time to talk,' he said.

'But I want to know what the charges are and what your defence will be. Surely we need to meet in your office before then?' I asked.

'OK,' he agreed flatly with a sigh, 'Make it one hour before the trial outside the court. Don't worry about anything; you would not be out on bail if the charges were serious.'

I was uneasy about such a short and late meeting, but there seemed no alternative. Perhaps he was right; possibly I was making a mountain out of a molehill.

'Do you want an interpreter at the trial? It will cost you 3000 Dirhams.'

I thought this was a very high price for Morocco, but could not imagine going to court without one, so I agreed. Later in the day he phoned to confirm that the trial had been delayed until Friday.

The following days felt surreal. We were free, yet did not want to go anywhere. There seemed to be no specific prohibition on travelling, although we were told by the port police not to go outside the province. I protested at this, as all the embassies were in the capital, Rabat, which was quite some distance from the Tetouan province. We did not appear to be followed, except in the port, but it was difficult to be sure. Two friends visited from Ceuta, and we prepared ourselves mentally for the case, even though we did not know what the charges were to be or what to expect.

In some respects, the rest of the week passed as if nothing had happened. Matti and Veikko busied themselves in cleaning and painting the yacht. They had been unsuccessful in contacting their Ambassador. Jacques was able to talk to the French Consul, who visited him at the apartment. I attempted to talk with Jacques, who seemed to know more about the case following this visit, but he seemed reluctant to discuss it with me. It was much later that I discovered that he had been advised by his lawyer and the French Consul to protest his innocence, and to allow the blame to be placed on me.

I made a phone call to a friend in the States who I had met at the Malaga conference. She was a lawyer to a Senator. She assured me that if things got difficult, I could call on outside support.

Two days before the trial, Matti and Veikko decided to go on a trip to the beautiful nearby village of Chefchouen, high in the Rif Mountains. We called a taxi and I negotiated a price and jokingly warned them about the drug barons who would be there to hassle them to purchase *hashish*. On their return in the evening, I happened to be watching as they were followed into the port by another vehicle, which pulled up behind their taxi. After paying the fare, the driver of the following car jumped out, and taking a uniformed police officer who was standing nearby, followed them to the yacht. I guessed that they had probably been tailed for the entire journey. I knew from past experience that this often happened. The officer called out to me asking where they had been.

I told him it was none of his business, 'They are tourists. If you want to know anything, ask them, not me!'

An argument broke out between two officers. I told them I would only talk with the chief of the port, not with them. I instructed Matti to return to the yacht while I sorted out the problem, and walked off to the marina office ignoring shouts from the officers telling me to stop. Once there, I complained to the duty police chief that my friends had been followed to Chefchouen and were now being hassled here in the port. To my amazement, the officer, a real gentleman, apologized and said that it would not happen again. It didn't, at least not to us.

A marina worker visited the yacht the next day and asked if I would like to have a phone.

'No, I have my mobile,' I told him.

He pointed out that only calls would be charged, not the line. Matti said he would not mind one, so I accepted the offer. He soon returned with a new telephone, attached to a long wire, and handed it to me on the fore-deck. I passed it down through the hatch and went below to check for a dialling tone while the fellow plugged it in on the jetty.

'It works,' I told him. Matti was soon talking to his wife in Canada.

An hour or so later, a black BMW saloon parked at the end of the jetty, and a smart-looking man in a suit came to the yacht with a cardboard carton in his hand.

He told me: 'I have a new replacement phone for you Captain.'

Guessing what was going on, I told him, 'I am happy with the phone we have and do not want to change it, thanks.'

He became indignant, insisting that he had to change it. I talked with Matti and told him, 'This should be fun; we are about to be bugged!'

We decided to allow the exchange and a swap was done. The 'new' phone was taped up at the side, with two extra wires leading from its base.

Passing the replacement phone through the hatch again to Matti, I went below and put a small transistor radio next to it, and tuned in to a Spanish sports station. Next we placed an inverted plastic bucket over the top, covering it with a towel to muffle the sound. We stood back laughing and admired our work, taking a photograph of the arrangement. Several hours later Matti, who slept in the forward cabin, said he could hear it ringing above the faint muffled sound of the radio. He picked up the receiver and was informed that there may be a fault on the phone.

'We are perfectly happy with it,' he laughed and hung up, turning the radio back on and replacing the bucket.

Some days later while visiting the office I was asked why I was not using the phone.

I told the secretary, 'You know, the new one they brought is such a disgusting colour! If they gave us back the original one, I will use it.'

She said she was unaware it had been changed. I told her the story of the visit by a police officer with the 'new' phone, and said that if the police shared the cost of the calls then I would be happy to use it. She laughed, obviously knowing what was going on.

10. The Trial

Friday 5th June 7am

Friday dawned, heralding the day of the trial. Again I awoke early. It was always difficult to get used to the two-hour time difference when the distance between Spain and Morocco was only a few miles. We had to be in court at eleven o'clock and I had arranged to meet the lawyer, Mr Abdullah, an hour earlier.

My wife and friends from Spain wanted to come over for the trial. It was a short ferry ride from Algeciras to Ceuta harbour and then only ten minutes to the frontier with Morocco. My friend would meet Anne and Ghada at the ferry terminal and would help them across the border. Since he lived in Ceuta he would have no difficulty crossing to Morocco. From there, it was half an hour to the marina.

The only real problem was crossing the frontier into Morocco. I had often stood for over an hour at the small window reserved for foreigners where passports were stamped. Even when there were only a few people waiting, we could often see the passport officer sitting at his desk chatting with his colleagues, but refusing to take passports from the sill behind the window. It was customary when this happened, to enclose cash in the passport in order to get some action. It seemed unfair, but so was the alternative of waiting.

As with nearby Gibraltar, Ceuta presents an uncomfortable political anomaly. The King of Morocco frequently calls for the two small provinces of Ceuta and Melilla to be reunited with his kingdom.

Like Gibraltar in the past, Ceuta thrives on smuggling across the border. Electronic goods purchased in Ceuta at greatly reduced and tax-free prices, are smuggled across the border into Morocco by the ton, while Moroccan wares are smuggled out: mostly marijuana and, these days, illegal immigrants. Every night many Africans creep over the mountain-top and descend into Ceuta in order to attempt the border crossing: one of the final steps to mainland Europe.

It was a bright, clear sunny day as we prepared ourselves for the court. I looked through the clothes hanging in the small wardrobe in my cabin, and realized I had nothing smart to wear. I wished I had thought of this earlier and could have asked Anne to bring over a jacket or even a suit. But it was too late now. She would have left home.

As the time approached to leave for Tetouan, Anne still had not arrived. Just as the deadline for our departure came, she arrived, seated in the front of an old, white Peugeot with Ceuta registration. It was a great sight. We embraced as Anne got out of the car with tears in her eyes.

Another friend whom I had not seen for some years, who lived nearby in Algeciras, had heard about our case and was also coming along with other friends. On their arrival at the marina, they hailed a passing taxi, while we departed on the half-hour journey for the rendezvous with the lawyers in the Peugeot.

We had arranged to meet in the car park opposite the court. This time we were attending a higher court, only a few hundred metres from the one we had visited following the interrogation, where we met with the King's Prosecutor. Parking the car we went in search of the lawyer, Abdullah, who told me he would be in a red Mercedes. We waited anxiously well past the appointed time for him to arrive.

Bouncing out of his car and seeing us, an obvious group of foreigners, Abdullah shouted out: 'Mr Graham?'

I was relieved to see him, as there was now only half an hour to spare before the case was due to be heard. He was a balding stocky man in his forties. He pulled out his briefcase from the boot of the car, along with a black cape and hurried into the court without saying more. I tried to follow him as he disappeared up a flight of stairs, but without success. There were hundreds of people pushing and shoving inside the building, with little apparent control from the police, who were everywhere. He remained in the building for around fifteen minutes while I anxiously awaited his return.

At last Abdullah appeared at the front door of the courtroom, and spotting me, bounded over shouting, 'We have plenty of time, the court is running late as usual.'

My other friends had just arrived, so we set off for a nearby café. As we walked I asked, 'What are the charges and what do you expect to happen?'

He said that he had not been informed of the exact charges.

'Don't worry, this is a simple case and will be dismissed. It is only a minor customs offence.'

I was extremely anxious and asked, 'How could you possibly have formed a defence, if you do not even know the charges?'

'Trust me,' he replied indignantly stopping to face me, 'I know what I'm doing.'

We entered a noisy café and sat at the far end, at the only empty table. Abdullah ordered mint tea for everyone. He then asked what had happened. I explained that my Finnish-Canadian friend had been taking some Bibles to the French national, Jacques, and had been stopped by the police, in the port of Marina Smir.

'OK,' he said. 'We will tell the judge that your friend took the books to Jacques because you were going to visit other places in Morocco and that you intended to collect them later on your return – OK?'

'But why such a story?' I asked. 'This is not true, and we did nothing wrong.'

'Look,' he replied 'do you want my help or not?'

I told him that we needed his help, but asked why it was necessary to tell such a story, which was untrue.

'You have to trust me, I am your lawyer!'

This, I came to realize, was his 'jingle' – I was to hear this phrase repeated over and over again in the coming months.

'Well, what would you like to say instead to the judge?' he asked.

'Why can't we tell the truth?' I asked. 'We were taking them to Jacques, who wanted to give them as gifts.'

'Why then did you enter the country illegally?' he asked.

I smiled and pulled out my passport to show him the entry stamp for 29th May, without saying a word. He looked at this and his eyes widened in amazement.

'Do you all have stamps?'

Veikko and Matti triumphantly showed him their stamped passports.

He sat shaking his head and rubbing his chin for some moments without saying anything.

Jacques and Françoise were with their lawyer a few tables away and I knew that they too had valid immigration stamps. They had entered Morocco from Ceuta in their camper the previous month, after spending two days collecting provisions.

'Well, what shall we tell the judge? Do you accept my defence?' he again asked.

As I hesitated, he stood up and said, 'You talk about it with your friends and give me your decision.'

At that he walked off to chat with Jacques' lawyer.

One friend immediately shouted indignantly, 'Tell the truth, you should not use that ridiculous story.'

I agreed and asked what Matti thought. He was less sure. 'Perhaps the lawyer knows best.'

I agreed, saying that it was possible that he had worked something out with the judge in advance of the trial, possibly during his brief time inside the court on his arrival. It seemed obvious that he knew more than he was telling us. But how much? It was many months later that I realized the extent of my naivety.

I reasoned with Matti that if we used the lawyer's story and were still convicted of some heinous crime, I would feel forever guilty, knowing that a false story had been presented under oath. On the other hand, if we were convicted, having told the truth, at least I could feel proud to have been condemned with my friends for being in possession of Bibles. This was agreed by all. I finished my mint tea and went over to the lawyer to tell him that I needed to speak with him.

Abdullah returned to our table, and before telling him of our decision, I described to him how we were made to sign papers in Arabic that we did not understand.

'Yes, I know,' he said.

I told him I had not signed mine on either occasion, and asked if the signature of the others would cause a greater problem for me.

He looked quizzically at me and asked, 'You had more than one paper to sign?'

I told him of the two separate days of interrogation and the two *Procès Verbals*. He again looked puzzled and said that this was impossible: we must be mistaken. Ignoring his disbelief, I then told him that nothing had been translated, and that we had not been allowed food or water for two days while the documents were compiled. He looked at the floor and responded apologetically, 'Yes, this is common.'

We could have insisted on an interpreter during the interrogation, he told us, but if we had done so, it could have meant waiting in the cells for weeks for one to become available. Although it was our legal right, it was usually very difficult to find one, as no qualified interpreter wants to work in the interrogation centre. This confirmed what the police had said, although I did not believe them at the time.

Returning to the subject of the papers, which he confirmed was the *Procès Verbal*, he said that if this was not signed, it could not be used in court. I asked if he had a copy of the document, and he answered that he did not, but he had requested one.

'Don't worry, the case will be dismissed,' he assured us. Then he continued to reassure us that we had not committed any crime against the law, and therefore should not worry about anything. We were all relieved to hear that as we left for the court. Once again, I was feeling high and confident.

'We have decided to tell the judge the truth,' I told him.

'OK, that is your decision,' he replied.

As we walked to the courthouse, I talked with Anne and expressed my distrust of the system. Here we were about to stand trial, and we still did not even know what the charges were. The lawyer did not seem to know much either, although it was obvious that he understood more than he was willing to say. I supposed, therefore, that he was also aware in advance that the case would be dismissed, as he said. He seemed very certain about that. Perhaps this was why he had not explained things. It was simply unnecessary for us to know. I managed to convince myself and felt elated as we entered the court.

We pushed our way through the crowds to move towards a room at the end of the first floor. Looking over the heads of the people crowding around the entrance, trying to push their way inside, we could see rows of benches with every seat occupied and many people standing. There was a terrific din coming from within and the heat and smell rolling out through the doors was stifling. Abdullah, with his head down, pushed his way into the courtroom through the crowd and disappeared. He soon emerged looking dishevelled, and informed us that our case would not be heard for a while.

We had been chatting outside for half an hour when a group of people emerged from the court. Abdullah returned, looked inside, and pulled me behind him. The others followed us in. Françoise and Jacques quickly managed to find two empty seats, while their lawyer made his way to the front. We were standing squashed against the side of the courtroom, along with about ten other people. Frequent commotions and numerous interruptions followed. The three judges on the front bench had to stop proceedings to ask the court ushers and uniformed police officers to remove the trouble-makers.

Soon another group left, and space was available for Anne and me to sit down. It seemed to go quiet in the court as we shuffled along the hard wooden bench. Soon our names were called and the two lawyers beckoned us to the front. We had to push our way past the people lining the sides. The lawyer had brought an interpreter, who stood behind me.

The judges – if that is what they were – seemed remarkably young. The central figure appeared to be in his thirties, while the two on either side were younger. I attempted eye contact with them, trying to establish their attitude to us. Those on either side of the central figure seemed totally disinterested. One sat with his head cupped in his hand and his elbow on the desk, looking bored. The other was shuffling through papers. Neither of them looked in our direction. The principal man in the centre looked studiously at a pile of papers spread out in front of him, which I could see were those presented to us for signing: the *Procès Verbal*. Of course, there was no way I could know if he was looking at the first or second version, nor to which of us it related.

Finally the central judge glanced down from the bench at Abdullah and nodded, indicating that he should begin. He launched into a speech, which the interpreter, standing behind me, began to translate.

'There is no case to answer. No criminal activity has been cited: the *Procès Verbal* cannot be used in court as it was not signed by the defendant and was not translated or read to him …'

Suddenly Abdullah was halted by the judge, who pointed to the interpreter and told him to be silent and to sit down.

Abdullah protested and, with the interpreter still talking in my ear, said, 'These people do not know Arabic and it is their right in accordance with the law to know the proceedings. This man is a qualified sworn court interpreter.'

The man continued to translate softly behind us, until he was told again sternly by the judge that this was forbidden, and he had to sit down. We understood nothing more of the proceedings, except when questions were addressed directly to us towards the end of the hearing.

Abdullah was asked to continue. After several minutes of listening to him in full flow, with arms flailing as if he was appearing in a Shakespearean play, he abruptly finished his presentation and motioned to Jacques and Françoise's lawyer to step forward. He gave a similar, though much less dramatic presentation. Suddenly, he too was finished and stepped back. The three judges huddled together and spoke in whispers to each other. I strained to pick up some of their conversation, but could hear nothing.

The central judge turned to the lawyer, saying a few words. He then pointed to the interpreter, who stood once again behind me and said, 'The judge asks what you were doing with those books in your possession.'

'I was not found with any books in my possession, Sir,' I explained.

'But your friend was,' he responded.

'They were presents: gifts for our French friend and I had no idea that they could possibly be a problem in Morocco, as I knew that they are not illegal in other Arab countries.'

'How do you know that?' he asked.

'I have visited many places,' I replied.

Once again the three men on the bench huddled together, looking at the papers on the desk and speaking quietly to each other. The judge then addressed Jacques, asking the same questions through his lawyer. I did not understand the answers he gave, but found out later that he had told the judge that I had brought the books in, and that Matti had taken them to his apartment.

Finally the judge looked at me and asked, whilst nodding in the direction of the interpreter, 'Do you have anything to say?'

'Yes,' I said, 'I am sorry for any inconvenience this has caused, but we genuinely did not know there was any problem or law against the Bible in Morocco. I take responsibility for what happened.'

I went on to tell him that I loved Morocco and its people and had been visiting for thirty years.

'I am here to finish my book, which your government Tourist Ministry knows about,' I concluded. He gave no acknowledgement or expression that conveyed what he thought. He turned to the lawyers, and without saying anything, motioned with his arm to indicate that we were dismissed.

We made our way to the door at the side of the courtroom. The court seemed to have suddenly emptied although I had not been aware of any movement.

Once outside, Abdullah, wiping the sweat from his brow, insisting: 'Everything is OK. Your statement was very good. It will be accepted by the judge: you will be leaving Morocco tonight if you wish, but I hope you stay and enjoy Morocco. It is a wonderful country!'

I asked him, 'Are you sure we will be completely free?'

'Trust me, I am your lawyer!'

Juan from Algeciras, who was standing nearby, agreed.

'He is right, you should have faith and believe it. Everything will be fine.'

I began to feel happy and thought of the trip out of the marina. We had been here for a week, but so much had happened that it felt much longer. The lawyer told us that we would normally have to wait a few days for the judgement.

'I have asked for a special dispensation and we will receive the judgement in an hour. Go, eat and celebrate, it is lunch-time,' he told us looking at his watch.

I had been up and down like a yo-yo for days and was not prepared to celebrate until we had heard the verdict.

The interpreter came over and asked if we still needed him. I had not realized that he was still there and apologized that he had not been allowed to interpret in court, adding that it was almost a wasted journey for him. He said it was most unusual and unfair for the judge to forbid it, but requested his payment. I asked how much he wanted, expecting a reduced amount, since he had not done much. He asked for the sum previously agreed with Abdullah – 3000 Dirhams ($300). I did not have the cash with me and so asked Abdullah if he would advance it, adding it to my account. He agreed to this.

As we walked away from the court to find somewhere to sit, I reflected on the morning's proceedings. On balance, it was most likely that the lawyer was right. The court had agreed/to deliver the judgement within the hour, rather than in a few days. Surely this could only mean that it had already been decided? How else could the lawyer be so certain of the outcome?

He had been so sure when he stated categorically, 'Tonight you will be free to leave Morocco with your boat, if you want to.'

Surely they would not risk a hasty negative judgement on foreigners? With that, I tried to put the whole thing out of my mind for an hour, while we awaited the verdict.

11. The Verdict

Friday 5th June 11am

We sat in the bright sunshine at a roadside café, where cheap plastic tables spilled out onto the pavement, as cars passed by only a few feet from us. These roadside cafés usually served the best mint tea. The waiter occasionally came out with a pot of water, which he threw on the pavement to keep the dust down.

As we waited for the tea to arrive in the traditional small glasses, I felt totally drained and aware that several of my friends were trying to converse with me. I was close to a breakdown and I knew it. I believed that my only security and protection was within my own mental wall. I felt guilty that these friends had travelled from Spain to support me during the trial, and I did not even feel able to engage in conversation with them. With so many letdowns, I was determined not to allow optimism to raise my hopes, and did not want to be talked into a false sense of security.

After an hour we paid for the tea and wandered in the direction of the court. Abdullah disappeared inside to find out if the verdict had been announced, fastening his white tuck collar and swinging his thick black pleated cape over his shoulder as he went. We followed him in to escape the blazing sun, which was hurting my eyes, in spite of the sunglasses I was wearing. We remained on the lower floor, while he went up the stairs. After a while I caught sight of him standing with a group of other lawyers and we all joined him. He soberly informed us that the customs authorities were asking for a thirty thousand Dollar fine and confiscation of the yacht and my motor scooter.

I felt devastated and overwhelmed, hardly capable of believing this further addition to the roller-coaster ride.

Cheerily, he added, 'Don't worry, this is normal in Morocco. It will result in a fine of 1,000 Dirhams, no more. You will be free today as I told you, trust me.'

I did not trust him, feeling that he must have known this information before, but had withheld it from us.

I began to argue, 'But even now we do not know what the charges are. You keep telling us that we had done nothing against the law!'

Ignoring me, he continued conversing with his legal friends. Was he trying to warn us bit by bit?

I felt sick in my stomach as I leaned against the wall of the lower courtyard for another hour, while we watched lawyers, judges and policemen come and go. My visiting friends tried to lift my spirits, reminding me that we had been given every assurance that all would be well. Abdullah, after all, did know the law and how this court functioned. Furthermore, there did not seem to be any charges, only what was alluded to by the King's Prosecutor: 'A minor indiscretion'. Even that was not mentioned in court, as far as we knew.

'Don't look so miserable!' they kept telling me.

Matti and the others said nothing. When asked, they sounded optimistic, but I wondered if they were harbouring similar doubts to mine.

It was a strange and new situation to be in. All my life, I have been criticized for being a crazy and incurable optimist, often achieving what others consistently told me were impossible goals. Now, I simply could not feel any grounds for optimism and did not even want to be persuaded. It was undoubtedly a reaction: an unconscious safety mechanism. I was very aware and afraid of my psychological state, and needed at all costs to protect myself.

I had no control over these circumstances, and knew that there was nothing I could do. So far, I had found these emotional ups and downs in response to news or expectations to be very draining and destructive. From now on, I was determined not to allow myself the luxury of feeling high until given definite reasons. I was losing my grip.

Graham Hutt in front of his lawyer's office in Tanger.

Finally, sweating profusely, Abdullah swept back down the stairs with Jacques' lawyer behind him, removing his collar and cloak as he did so.

When he reached the bottom step, he announced, 'The news is not good, but don't worry, we can appeal.'

There was silence. I was reluctant to hasten the bad news. After a moment's pause to get his breath back, while he again mopped the sweat from his forehead, he continued in a low serious voice.

'You have been sentenced to a prison term of two months and a fine of 420,000 Dirhams.'

'Furthermore, your yacht has been confiscated, along with your motor scooter. Also the camper van belonging to Jacques (in which they found more books – this was the first time I had heard about that) is to be handed over to the customs authorities. Françoise has been found not guilty and she is free to leave Morocco.'

Open mouthed, we gasped.

Juan spoke first. 'This is impossible!'

'I am very sorry,' replied Abdullah. 'They should not have done this. There were no charges presented and no customs officers were in court to give any evidence against you. This is against the due process of law and justice. I have never, in all my time practising as a lawyer, seen such an injustice in my country. I am ashamed.'

This quote later appeared in the international press after he repeated it to a reporter.

He then told us, 'The prison sentences are suspended, pending the payment of the fine.'

'How could this have happened?' I asked him. 'How could they have arrived at a sentence, increased far beyond what the prosecutor was calling for, and way beyond even what the customs authorities were demanding? What exactly were the charges?' I asked.

'I have never known this to happen before, and do not understand any of it.'

He elaborated, 'The judges are young and perhaps they have never had to deal with a case like this. They are used to dealing with petty drug offences.'

'To whom does the sentence apply?' I enquired. 'Are we all to receive the suspended prison sentence, or just me? Why was Veikko convicted when he had nothing to do with it? Only Matti was found with books.'

Although we were pleased for Françoise to be let off, I asked, 'How can she be considered less culpable than Veikko? She was in exactly the same position.'

He said the fine was calculated at five per cent of the value of the books, and was applied to me, and that Françoise was a woman.

Making a rough calculation, I said, 'That makes the Bibles worth more than a million Dollars! How could they possibly value a few Bibles at a figure of over a million Dollars? That's ridiculous!'

Abdullah said he had no idea how they came up with such a figure, but we could contest it if we chose to appeal.

He then elaborated on the sentence, 'You are the one held to blame,' he said.

'But', I protested, 'the main bulk of books were found in Jacques' apartment, and there were books also in his camper that I knew nothing about! Since none of this was raised in court, where did they get their information?'

He shrugged his shoulders.

'Did the court simply accept my willingness to take the blame for the books?'

He replied that the whole process of law was flawed in this case, and should be contested.

Then it dawned on me. There must be information in the *Procès Verbal* that neither we, nor the lawyer, had any idea about.

'Could this be true? Did they use the *Procès Verbal*?' I asked.

Abdullah, avoiding the question, said quietly, 'They should not have used it as evidence in court: it was not signed.'

'Yes, but was it used? Can we obtain a copy?' I asked impatiently.

He repeated that he did not have it and again said that it was unimportant since it could not be used in court. I responded angrily: 'The judge was reading from it! I could clearly see that this was the document spread out on the bench: I was standing only a few feet away and could see this was the document in front of him.'

He looked down and finally agreed, 'I will obtain a copy for you.'

Abdullah offered to arrange an appeal, as soon as possible.

'Are we allowed to return to the yacht?' I asked.

'No, it has been handed to the customs authorities by the court. It no longer belongs to you.'

He reiterated that the jail sentence was suspended pending the appeal process. My mind was racing. What were we to do?

'How long might it take to appeal?' I asked.

'It could be a long process, over a year,' he admitted, but said that he would ask for it to be brought forward.

'You could leave the country,' he suggested. 'In fact, you should.'

'But once we were out, we would never be allowed to return, even for the appeal,' I protested.

He insisted that this was not true, but I had read in the Spanish press of people involved in cases who were refused re-entry when they attempted to return to contest their sentence.

He suggested we go to a hotel to think about it.

'Will we at least be able to collect our belongings from the yacht?' I asked despondently.

'Only your personal belongings, nothing else.' he replied. 'The yacht is no longer yours.'

Everything seemed so final.

Anne tried to convince me to leave Morocco and to return to Spain with her, noting that I was not mentally fit enough to fight this without a break. I could feel anger mixed with a physical cramp rising from within, and I retreated back into my shell, while I worked out what to do. I decided to take as much as possible from the yacht and move into a cheap hotel that I knew in M'Diq.

Abdullah was still with us, continually wiping his forehead and shaking his head. He seemed as genuinely shocked as the rest of us. Was this another great actor? Jacques' lawyer was talking to him and Françoise in soft tones. I could hear several voices projecting towards me and offering advice, but could not make out any one person. They were merging into one strange, distant hollow sound. When I was a boy, I loved to hold a long cardboard tube to my ear and listen to the amplified and distorted sounds echoing down the tube. The sounds I now heard were like listening through that tube. The voices were well-meaning, but I was too paralysed to respond, unable to process the information coming my way. Perhaps Anne was right, but I could not leave until I had seen this through to the finish.

My head cleared, and I told Abdullah to prepare an appeal, since we had nothing to lose and everything to gain. Then I announced that under no circumstances would I leave Morocco, as I felt sure we would not be allowed to return once out of the country.

'Yes, you are right,' he now agreed, despite his earlier denials.

Jacques, Françoise, Veikko and Matti put their hands on my shoulders, and agreed that we would all stick together until the end. I felt tears welling up and a cramp over my entire body. Still dazed, we wandered out into the street. Juan, the pastor friend visiting from Algeciras, asked if he could pray for us. We agreed and stood in a small circle while he did so, asking God for our protection and to give us wisdom.

As we journeyed back to the yacht, I was totally absorbed as I attempted to sort out priorities of what to do next. I decided I would take off everything of value, or at least as much as we were allowed. We stopped at the hotel in M'Diq to make a reservation, telling the receptionist that I would return with our luggage later. For the first time, I became aware that the familiar faces I saw sitting around in the hotel lobby were police officers trying to look like tourists. As we left the hotel to drive the short distance to the yacht, I told myself not to get too paranoid about such things.

12. Return to the Yacht

Friday 5 June 3pm

As we drew into the marina, hitting the same pot-hole that laid in wait for us before, I felt a wave of disgust for this country and its people, something I had never sensed before. How could they have tried us, without allowing us to know what the charges were, or what was happening in the court? How was it that even the lawyer did not seem to have any idea of what was going on? Were we naive or just stupid for not accepting the story he suggested as our defense? Would it have made any difference? How could I find out the truth and fight back?

Despite having slowed to a walking pace, the car bottomed out with a loud scraping noise as the exhaust system hit the final speed hump. All was quiet, with two policemen puffing on cigarettes and pacing aimlessly in the large, empty car park. We neared the quay and made our way towards the yacht. As we did so we saw several police and customs officials walking towards us from the office building, obviously having seen our arrival. I told the others to climb aboard quickly and gather up as many of their possessions as possible.

Mohammed, the chief, bounded over and asked me what the verdict was. I responded that I was not really sure, but in any case, we would appeal.

'You are not allowed on the yacht. It has been confiscated,' he stated.

'Nothing is certain until the appeal, and in any case,' I told him, 'I want my belongings.'

He did not argue.

Jacques and Françoise wandered off in the direction of their apartment while I stepped on board and waited to see what would happen next. To my astonishment, no one tried to stop me. Descending below, we began hastily to gather our personal luggage. I stuffed some of my favourite CDs into a bag, as well as my satellite navigation computer and VHF radio equipment. I looked through the ship's papers, taking the most important documents.

We emerged with our luggage to a crowd of waiting police and customs officers.

One shouted something I could not understand. Mohammed translated: 'You cannot take anything with you!'

I said it was personal stuff and invited him to take a look. Mohammed became engaged in an argument with the customs officer, who then wandered off.

We loaded the bags into the back of the car, and a scruffy man in plain clothes said we needed to go to their office to get clearance before we could leave. I looked him up and down and asked him who he thought he was. He looked embarrassed and another officer explained that this was a senior customs officer. I asked him his name, but he would not give it.

Why not go back onto the yacht and refuse to leave? What would the police actually do about it? I talked with Veikko and Matti about this, and suggested that we had nothing to lose by attempting to remain on board. If they stayed here while I checked into a hotel with Anne, we could gauge the reaction.

I offered to sort out the bags and bring back anything they needed, if we found it possible to stay on the yacht. The rest of the gear could either go to Spain with the friends who came for the trial, or be stored at the hotel until someone could take it over the border. They happily agreed and boarded the yacht. I shouted to them to stay below, and to tell anyone who tried to remove them that they had orders from the captain not to leave until he returned.

Then I got into the car and we drove slowly to the customs office. The officers were not there, but a policeman came out, and asked us to open the boot. As we did so, he looked over the top of the car towards the customs office and said softly: 'OK. Leave quickly.' I closed the boot, and we drove out of the marina. First we went to the hotel, checked in and got the key to the room, which was particularly dismal, with rotting net curtains and a hard bed. The skirting board was chipped and the bathroom was filthy, but at least it was a place to store things, if nothing else. This would be a good half-way-house, somewhere I could stay with Anne, while attending the boat and getting more gear off – just in case.

I now had two plans to work on. The first was to stay as long as possible on the yacht, hoping that we could remain until an appeal released us. The second was to remove as much gear from the yacht as possible, anticipating a time when we may be forcibly removed or forbidden to return. We re-organized the bags, sorting out items that could be left and those that were not immediately needed. We then drove to the border with the owner of the car and two other friends from Spain.

Jacques insisted that Françoise left, while he stayed on for the appeal.

On the way to the border, the car owner offered to lend me his Peugeot to use in Morocco for as long as necessary. This was a real bonus now that we did not have a vehicle. My scooter, which I always carried on board, had been confiscated by the court and was in the hands of the customs authorities in the marina. This kind gesture lifted my gloomy spirits as we journeyed. Once at the border, my friends carried the large bags, full of heavy yacht equipment, from the boot of the car, and across the border into Ceuta.

I returned with Anne to the hotel in M'Diq and asked her to look after the room, while I went on to the yacht for a few hours, to check on the Canadians. To my surprise, when I arrived in the marina, there were no officers to be seen. I parked near the yacht, expecting them to come out, but still no one came. I spotted two officers getting up from a bollard they were sitting on, but they did not come my way. I got out and locked the car. Before stepping on board, I loosened the two bow ropes to allow the yacht to drift further away from the quay: just enough to make it difficult to step aboard, unless you were used to it. I managed the stretch from the quay to the anchor, which nestled in its bracket at the front, and clambered on.

Matti's head popped out of the hatch as I walked along the deck to take up the slack on the stern lines, created by my releasing the bow ropes. At first he looked worried, until he realized it was me. I asked him what had happened.

'Did any officers come round to tell you to leave?'

'One came and told us to go, but I ignored him,' he said.

We talked about our situation, and he pledged, on behalf of himself and Veikko, that they would stay in Morocco and see this through to the end. He also said that he needed to try to change his return ticket to Canada, which was for a flight departing from Malaga airport during the following week.

Rather amazed but pleased that we were still on board, I was uncertain how long it could last. Could we simply hold out on the yacht until the appeal, I wondered? We broke out some cans of beer and celebrated our return. Not much to celebrate, perhaps, but at least we were actually back aboard.

I realized how important it would be to ensure that at least one person was always on the yacht. If there was no one, the customs authorities could immediately take the opportunity to move it to another location nearer their office, where they had more control. They had power to do this and I could not understand why they were not enforcing their authority. It made no difference; I would exploit the situation anyway.

Two or three hours later, I heard the all too familiar: 'Captain, captain!' My heart plummeted, as I peered out of the hatch towards the bows of the yacht, and saw a customs officer standing there. He shouted something in Arabic, then in French. I knew that he was signalling for us to leave. I shrugged my shoulders and returned below. He shouted again, but I ignored him.

Half an hour later there was another shout. This time I recognized the voice as belonging to Mohammed. He was on the jetty with the same customs officer.

'You have to leave the boat,' he commanded in English.

With a look of surprise, I shouted back, 'This is my boat, and I have no intention of leaving it!'

He spoke to the customs officer and then repeated his demand for me to leave.

'Why? I asked.

'The court has given the yacht to the customs authorities' he replied.

'No,' I retorted, 'this could not possibly be true. Nothing is certain until after the appeal has taken place.'

Once again, he spoke with the customs officer, this time in an argumentative tone of voice and waving his arms. Together they wandered off, shouting at each other as they went.

One more attempt was made by a customs officer that day to get me to leave. This time, he drew his pistol and waved it towards me. I could see it was a half-hearted gesture, so I laughed at him as I raised my hands mockingly. The police officer accompanying him also laughed. The customs officer soon left, leaving the policeman still smiling in my direction.

I took the opportunity to ascertain the extent of a division between them by moving along the deck to thank him. To my great delight, he held out his hand to shake mine. Looking in the direction of the customs officer, who was by now several metres away, he spoke a few words under his breath that I could not understand. I knew he was making some insulting comment about him, and realized there was indeed a rift between the two forces. I would be able to exploit this over the coming months.

I stayed on board until evening, aware that the marina would then begin to fill with local people, who came at night to wander around and visit the disco. I planned to leave for the hotel to write e-mails and have dinner with Anne. It was with some fear that I prepared to go to M'Diq after dark, leaving Matti and Veikko on board with the same instruction as before – on no account leave the yacht. There was plenty of food and water on board, so I had few concerns for them. Possibly I could be prevented from coming back. I jumped the larger gap from the front of the yacht to the jetty, and walked to the car, expecting to be followed, but in fact there was no indication that I was being pursued.

I almost tripped over the guardian who was squatting in the darkness close to the end of the quay, as I neared the car. There were at least ten of these night 'guardians' employed by the marina. They saw everything and were instructed to report any unusual activity in the port to the uniformed police. Since the marina was empty of any yachts, almost any activity was unusual. I had struck up a friendship with this fellow on a previous visit, and remembered him telling me in Spanish how little they were paid for the twelve-hour night shift. I had given him cigarettes and some food.

I greeted him and he immediately stood up and beamed, putting two fingers to his lips in a gesture requesting a cigarette, obviously remembering me. I told him to wait while I returned to the yacht. I collected some fruit, cheese, bread and a packet of cigarettes: I always carried a ready supply. When I returned, he beamed with gratitude, as I handed these to him in a bag. I mentioned that I was going for a drive and he promised to look after my yacht, touching his eye with a finger.

He asked where I was going.

I answered, 'Anywhere the wind is blowing.'

He chuckled as I got into the car. I guessed he would be obliged to report the conversation to the police.

There was virtually no traffic on the road as I returned to M'Diq. Different plain-clothed policemen now occupied the chairs in the reception area. I was beginning to recognize all their faces.

I met up with Anne in our room, and we decided where to eat. Although I was reluctant to leave the hotel room unattended, I thought it would be more suspicious if we never left. We ate in a cheap local fish restaurant where the food was wonderful and cost the equivalent of one US Dollar. Returning to the hotel later, I downloaded my e-mails and updated friends around the globe of our current situation. I simply could not face staying at the hotel, wondering what was happening on the yacht. I discussed this with Anne, and we finally decided to take the computer and return to the yacht, but to leave our belongings in the room. They were mostly clothes and would not be missed if they were tampered with. As we left I took the precaution of retaining the room key so that it would be less obvious in reception that we were not around.

We arrived at the yacht to the delight of Matti and Veikko. I had to slacken off the stern lines to enable Anne to climb on board. She made tea, and we talked until the early hours.

It was a sombre time as we discussed the trial, the sentence, the possibility of going to prison, how to fight the case and the feeling of injustice. If we were really charged with a customs violation, then how could it have ended with such an incredibly harsh sentence? Even if there should have been duty paid on the books, which I knew was not the case, we would only have been guilty of avoiding payment of a few Dirhams. Every day during the summer months, hundreds of vehicles cross the border from Ceuta into Morocco, laden with undeclared goods.

The goods brought in from Europe are sold in Morocco to subsidize the vacation, and to buy gifts for their families. It is well known that customs officers prefer to take *baksheesh* and then allow the cars through without charging duty. Few declare anything, and even if they are apprehended for not making a declaration, or for not paying *baksheesh*, they are only fined a small amount before being allowed to continue on their journey.

Why was our treatment so different? What was really going on?

13. The Truth Unfolds

Saturday 6th June 8am

I awoke having had the first good sleep for several nights. The fact that we had been allowed to stay on board, despite attempts to dislodge us, was encouraging. Over the weekend there were more feeble attempts to remove us by the customs officers, who were usually accompanied by a police officer for translation purposes. But it was obvious that there was no serious intention behind their words. I could not understand why there was not more action. The yacht was clearly no longer mine, according to the judge's order, but I had nothing to lose by continuing to stake my claim on it. I fully intended to persist until forced off.

The weekend was peaceful with just a single yacht from Gibraltar entering the port for one night only. It gave me the idea that if it seemed like we were going to be forced off, I could ask a friend in Spain to come over with his yacht, and take away some of the more valuable items I was carrying on board. These included my life-raft, large amounts of rope, and the Zodiac dinghy and outboard motor.

We were moored near two restaurants, El Gaucho and a Chinese eating-place. Both seemed to be closed most of the time. Another, right opposite the yacht, became our haunt as it served the best, though initially expensive, mint tea. We got to know the owner and his staff, who were very friendly. It was not long before they were inviting us over for tea, rarely accepting payment.

It became clear from our conversations that, as I suspected, the police who had initially arrested us were now siding against the customs officers who were pressing to take the yacht. A high official had seen my yacht on previous visits and wanted it. He was determined to find any excuse to get it. This added yet another new and unexpected dimension to the case. The restaurant owner told me that he had seen articles in the local press about our case, stating that we had come into Morocco to: 'Undermine the Islamic faith, as subversives'. It became something of a joke with him as we pretended to have concealed guns hidden under our shirts, ready to shoot if they did not immediately convert.

We became familiar with the routine of the marina. It did not take long to realize that nothing goes unobserved. During the weekdays the place was empty apart from the many police wandering around. Only in the evenings and at weekends did the marina come alive, filled with local Moroccan tourists who drove from M'Diq and Tetouan and who visited the shops and restaurants lining the main quay. The nearby golden beaches were similarly empty, except at weekends.

Anne had to go back to Spain on Sunday evening, as Ghada was due to return to school. We went to the hotel and collected most of the gear stowed there and filled some bags. Returning by way of the yacht, I sorted out more of the important items we would not need to take back to Spain. It was almost dark and the marina car park was full. Our friendly guardian looked on but said nothing, as we loaded the car before setting out on the short journey to the border at Ceuta. I told him that he would be rewarded when I returned.

The weekend seemed to have flashed past by the time Monday arrived. After dialling the British Embassy in Rabat many times and finding the line continually engaged, I was finally able to speak with an official. I asked if the embassy staff had been aware of the trial and its outcome. The Vice Consul had been informed, and she told me it was 'the expected result.' I was stunned! How could she possibly say that, when there had been only a minor customs violation that apparently had not even been referred to in court?

I did not argue, but asked for an appointment to see the Ambassador or at least the Consul. I was informed that I could visit, but that she thought it was an unnecessary journey. I wanted to make the case public, in order to get justice. This I was told would be a very foolish thing to do, inevitably resulting in negative consequences. Instead I should visit the second Consul, based in Tanger, who had visited me in Tetouan if I felt in need of any assistance.

The question of publicity was a delicate one as it had the potential to embarrass the Moroccan authorities: something I wanted to avoid, if at all possible. I decided to seek the advice of several other friends both in and outside of the country. I required more information about the charges we were convicted of, as we still had no idea, although we were by now hearing different stories. I was sure they could not possibly be for a minor customs violation because of the penalties imposed by the court.

Was it a case of religious persecution because it involved Bibles? Although there were no open accusations of a religious nature, I knew the consequences of proselytising in Morocco, and wondered if we had been convicted on this charge. The waiters implied that their reading of the local press and talk of subversion indicated that this was indeed the case. Foreigners on tourist visas accused of proselytising were usually expelled without going to court, but it was nevertheless considered a serious offence.

I needed to know what was in the *Procès Verbal*. Although not officially admitted as evidence in court according to the lawyer, it was obviously used to convict us, and had been open on the judge's bench during the trial. Who was actually culpable – all of us, or just me? Increasingly, hints suggested that it was me who was being blamed.

After contacting the embassy, I phoned my lawyer and arranged to visit him. His office was in Tanger, which I knew well. I wasted no time departing, stopping off at the hotel in M'Diq on the way through to check our remaining belongings. I was not sure that I still needed to retain the room, but it was cheap and made a good storage depot for additional items, which I might need to remove from the yacht.

The journey across the Rif Mountains is as spectacular as it is dangerous. The road is narrow and windy, with few places to overtake. High in the mountains, standing at the side of the road, are Berber women selling farm produce. Cheese, live chickens and seasonal vegetables make a truly interesting sight as these ladies, dressed in bright red and white striped dresses, energetically hold up their wares, hailing each passing motorist. I often tried to get a photograph of them, but it was almost impossible. Suspicious of the camera, they would hide.

Passing the small village of Ain Lassan, the smell of grilled lamb on the open-air barbecues was always too irresistible to pass without a brief stop.

As I travelled, I decided to phone the British Consul in Tanger to thank her again for the visit she paid me in

Tetouan. It was important to maintain the relationship just in case I needed her help again. I also considered visiting her while I was in the town.

'Did you hear about the outcome of our case?' I asked.

'Yes, you were lucky to get such a light sentence,' she replied.

'How can you possibly say that a fine and other penalties totalling almost 300,000 Dollars, along with a jail sentence, could be considered light for bringing in a few Bibles?' I asked in exasperation.

'This is Morocco. You could have been prosecuted for drug smuggling or, even worse, for proselytising and been handed out a six-year jail sentence!'

Amazed, I insisted that we were not charged with those crimes as far as I knew. She repeated, 'This is Morocco and you were foolish!'

I decided that there was obviously no point in visiting her.

Once in Tanger, I found Abdullah's office and parked the car in the narrow street. The appeal date had not yet been set; it might be at least three weeks before we would be informed when it was to take place.

'It is not unusual to wait a year for an appeal,' he reminded me as I sat across from his desk, 'but I will continue to press for the earliest possible date.'

He was reluctant to give me any information at all and seemed anxious to close the discussion.

I decided it might help if I explained to him that I had a doctorate in medical anthropology and a degree in psychology, and that I wanted to be informed in detail about what was going on.

'I know I do not have any legal qualifications,' I told him, 'but I think I have the capacity to follow what is going on. Please, Abdullah, be honest with me.'

At first he repeated that he did not know and had not received the court judgement. 'You will just have to wait,' he said, but then added: 'I have managed to obtain a copy of the *Procès Verbal*.'

Slowly opening up further, Abdullah admitted that there were several matters brought up in the court, which he said had indeed originated from the *Procès Verbal*. 'These should not have been raised, as you did not sign the document.'

I pressed for more information. He then mentioned the question of our illegal entry.

'The immigration authorities could not find you listed on their computer. Everyone coming into and leaving Morocco is listed there!' he told me, accusingly.

'It is obvious why we are not on the computer,' I told him. 'We came in by yacht. The formalities in the ports are done by hand as there are no computers in the small ports of Morocco! Are they blaming me for that?'

He was amazed and immediately recorded it on paper. I asked him to photocopy the page in my passport with the entry stamp so that he could furnish proof to the authorities that we had entered legally. He called his secretary, who took the passport to make a copy of the appropriate page. I then asked him what other charges were being made against me.

He then told me about some large study books – Bibles – that were found in cartons and mentioned in court. I knew nothing about these books and was surprised. After he described them, I realized that they were the ones that Jacques had brought in quite legally from his visits to Ceuta, where they were on sale. He had friends who wanted them.

'You are being held responsible by the customs for these, and for everything Jacques had in his possession,' he stated.

'Was I also to be held responsible for what Jacques had in his camper van?' I asked.

'Well, yes!' he told me.

Jacques's lawyer had apparently agreed that this was to be their story. Perhaps this was the reason Jacques was so reluctant to talk to me.

'Even if I had been responsible in some way for the books, what difference would it make, since there was nothing illegal?' I argued.

He then explained further that Jacques had been advised not to admit to bringing any of the books from Ceuta. I knew from seeing them at the police station that these books were large and were contained in their original cartons. But why would we carry large cartons from the yacht right under the noses of the police, who we knew were everywhere?

'I know, the notion is ridiculous.'

'There is even a military post less than ten metres from the French couple's apartment!' I told him.

I was surprised that Jacques had other Bibles in his apartment and my feelings about being blamed for these were mixed. On the one hand, I had already agreed to take the blame, but that was when I thought I knew exactly what was involved. I knew precisely what books had been found in Matti's possession and that nothing on the yacht could be considered illegal.

'We will appeal against these ridiculous charges,' I exclaimed, 'as they could easily be proved false.'

'No' he said. 'The appeal can only challenge the court process and proceedings – which had been violated – but not the evidence presented. This is the law of Morocco,' he explained.

'But the basic facts are wrong and there must surely be a way to correct these?' I protested.

'There is no way: this is the law,' he shrugged.

I was flabbergasted, and wondered what sort of legal system could possibly deny an investigation into elements of a case that could be proved to be false. I later learned that Morocco was not unique in this.

The situation became even more bizarre when I discovered many more incorrect statements that formed the basis of our judgement. None of these could be contested. Abdullah did assure me that there were so many breaches of the process of law and justice that no appeal court could uphold the sentence.

'The case will be quashed at the appeal. Don't worry; trust me!' he repeated yet again.

Should I make the case public? When I first mentioned this to Abdullah he said it would be a bad idea because it would anger the authorities. He sat and thought for a while, and then mentioned a case that had been reported in the Spanish newspapers as well as the international press.

At ninety-years-old, Si Mahdi was imprisoned for apparently explaining to an enquirer the facts about Christianity. The old man was of Moroccan parents but was an American citizen and a well-known local Christian. The enquirer had betrayed him to the police, claiming that he had tried to convert him. Abdullah admitted that if it had not been for the huge press coverage in America, he would have died in prison. Abdullah had been the lawyer representing Si Mahdi, who had spent many days in a freezing dungeon until he was finally released. He looked at me closely and said: 'Do what you think best; you have to decide.' My mind was almost made up.

Abdullah went on to say that there were several unusual features about our case. First, we were accused initially of bringing in Bibles, which was not an offence.

He told me that people were often charged with proselytising, but we were not.

'I just cannot understand why you were given bail,' he said. 'It is most unusual for someone in your position to be out on bail. They are usually kept in custody until a final outcome of the case is known.'

When I mentioned that we were back on the yacht, he was even more amazed.

'But you said we have done nothing against the law.'

'In all honesty, Christian books are considered more illegal than drugs in Morocco, even though there is no law against them,' he sighed.

He continued by saying that the authorities really did not know what to do with us or how to react. Ours was an extraordinary situation. Finally I asked Abdullah for a copy of the *Procès Verbal*. He agreed that I could collect a copy from him at the court, as he was due to be there again the following day.

While driving back to the marina, I made several phone calls to friends in Spain and in the United States, to ask their advice about making the case public. From these conversations I learned that another of my American friends, who worked in a Senator's office, had been the very lawyer who had brought the case of Si Mahdi to the attention of the American President. She reminded me that human rights issues are important to Americans and that Morocco is a signatory to international human rights agreements and receives financial aid as a result. Because of this, if agreements are violated, pressure can be exerted to bring about justice, especially if American citizens are involved.

Everyone I spoke with, apart from the British Embassy staff, advised me to make as much publicity as possible in order to get an early resolution. Even Abdullah had indicated that this could help me. My mind was made up as I journeyed back to the hotel.

As soon as I returned I wrote an e-mail with a full report of everything I had learned to date regarding the *Procès Verbal*, and its illegal use in court, at least as far as I could ascertain. I also wrote of the injustice of a legal system that convicted on false statements, which the accused had never seen, and that could not subsequently be contested at the appeal. I still needed evidence that this document was used to convict me and this was soon to come.

Meanwhile Matti and Veikko had been successful in contacting the Canadian Consul who agreed to visit them in the port. There was some confusion and mis-understanding about where the meeting would take place, but on the next day – Tuesday – Matti and Veikko went to Rabat to see her.

Later that Tuesday evening I saw a large vehicle bearing diplomatic registration plates slowly circling the port. I wandered over to see if it was the car from either the British or Canadian Embassy. The passenger in the back was the Canadian Consul. I apologized that Matti and Veikko were not aboard and told her that they thought the meeting was in Rabat. I was sure that they would soon return and offered to take her to the restaurant in the meantime. She agreed, and we went, together with the Consul's assistant, to order a snack.

I pressed the Consul for news and advice, but she insisted, 'I am really sorry, but I am not at liberty to say anything as you are not a Canadian Citizen.'

I nevertheless told her of my dissatisfaction with the way we had been treated by the authorities – we had not been permitted a lawyer during the interrogation, or food or water. No interpreter had been present during the interrogation and we had no idea what was written on the papers we were told to sign. Apparently this was normal practice in Morocco, even though it was against international law and unjust.

As time passed and the Canadians did not return, she volunteered, 'You know, you are in very serious trouble. I will be advising my nationals to get out of Morocco as soon as possible,' she said.

She then told me that she had been at the court in Tetouan for the past few hours and had managed to find out the contents of the *Procès Verbal*. I told her how I had tried to get a copy and said that even my lawyer did not have it during the trial, or at least that is what he told me. She was amazed at this news and seemed to think that Abdullah would have received a copy.

After some time, Matti and Veikko returned. We drank mint tea together with the Consul, who then asked them, 'Shall we sit somewhere and talk?' indicating that I should leave them to talk alone. I stood up to go, but to my delight, they insisted, 'No, please stay with us. We want you here if that is all right.'

The Consul beckoned me to sit down again. I began to take notes. She immediately reiterated to the others that she had been to the court with her assistant and had learned the contents of the *Procès Verbal*.

'The minor charges against you include illegal entry, avoiding immigration procedures and failing to declare your yacht and its contents on arrival. Further charges are those of subversion, attempting to overthrow the government of Morocco, and attempting to undermine Islam and the authority of the King.'

I gasped.

'There is more,' she informed us. Looking at Veikko and Matti she advised decisively: 'Get out of Morocco as quickly as possible!'

'But this is all lies,' Matti protested, pulling out his passport to show her the entry stamp.

After studying the page she turned to me and asked, 'Do you also have an entry stamp in your passport?'

'Of course, it is impossible to come here without one!' I exclaimed, taking my passport from my pocket and showing her the stamp.

By now I had memorized the page number it was on. Turning to me again she said, 'If you intend to stay, photocopy that page in your passport: it is very important. But my advice is that you too should get out immediately.'

Coming from an embassy official, this was particularly frightening and very dramatic. Then I remembered how, following the trial, Abdullah had also urged us to leave immediately, though without stating any reason.

'My yacht is here, and I want to fight against these false and ridiculous charges,' I told her.

She responded, 'Do you know what sort of a sentence you can get for these charges? You should not be worrying about your yacht, but your freedom!'

I was dumbfounded, remembering Abdullah's astonishment that we were out on bail, rather than in a cell. His reaction now made sense. I was convinced; he knew much, much more than he would tell me.

Although I knew how easy it was to walk across the border at Ceuta by bribing the police, it would be very dangerous for Veikko and Matti to leave Morocco without going through passport control. They could easily be arrested and be in far worse trouble.

I explained this to the Consul, who said, 'Don't worry about them. I am their diplomatic representative. I have ways of overcoming technical difficulties at the border.'

Matti immediately dismissed this idea and then told her that they preferred to stay and fight with me, as we were all in this together.

'Take a walk and discuss it on your own before making this hasty and rash decision,' she advised.

They departed into the darkness towards the yacht.

Just how serious was all this? There was absolutely no evidence for any of the charges she mentioned.

The Consul laughed and said there was no need of evidence. I told her how the *Procès Verbal* had been elicited and how the others had been intimidated into signing it, by assurances that we would all be released as soon as we had done so.

I also mentioned that Jacques and Françoise were elderly, and that Veikko was also old, and suffering from a heart condition.

'Yes,' she responded, 'all the more reason to get out, as the charges of subversion could take you into much deeper trouble, and the sentence could even be increased at the appeal hearing.'

I asked how this could be. 'Why were the sentences at the first hearing so light if these were the real charges?

She had no answer.

Nothing seemed to make sense.

'What is on paper is one thing,' she explained, 'but the judgement was taken on things unwritten. The *Procès Verbal* is an aid to the conviction since it is your "confession". This is a verbal culture.'

I understood well what she meant. The Arabic language is beautiful, reflecting the vast and ancient culture and religion. Stories are remembered without them being written down. Many ordinary Muslims have memorized the entire Qur'an and can recite it.

I suddenly realized that after all this talk of the charges and what action to take, she had not even mentioned the supposed 'real' cause of the arrest: the books!

'What about the Bibles?' I asked.

'Oh, that is a very minor issue, of no real consequence. The real problem you have is not from the Bibles, but the other charges, which are substantial,' she said.

I was left perplexed and more confused, but determined to clear my name, and to take my yacht out of Morocco. I told her that I had friends in the Moroccan government but had been reluctant, so far, to call them, since I could not believe that I was in any real trouble.

'Use any influence you can,' she advised. 'And be very careful when you travel.'

What were the consequences for me if the others left the country? She informed me that although we were all charged and found equally guilty, except Françoise, I was the one they blamed as the ringleader. If the others left the country it would not make any difference to my plight. I was sure she was right, but hoped I could get some assistance from my embassy, now that I had seen her in action and willing to do anything to help her nationals.

Veikko and Matti soon returned and asked me to join in their conversation. I took my leave of the Consul.

'We have decided to stay and fight the case with you as we originally planned,' said Matti.

'Well Matti,' I responded, 'if that is your decision, I appreciate it. But I am also aware of the danger you would be in if your bid to cross the border failed and you were arrested by the police there.'

They returned to the Consul, who had by now been with us for two or more hours since her arrival in the port. She informed them that she would be leaving for Rabat shortly.

'Please reconsider: it may be the most important decision you two will ever make,' she said.

'No, our minds are made up: we will stay here with Graham,' Matti said decisively.

She immediately stood up and said goodbye to Viekko and Matti as they departed back to the yacht, while I thanked her for her assistance. It was well past midnight as she was driven out of the port that night.

The truth had dawned: we really were in trouble! I had no idea how to fight a system that convicted on the basis of verbal statements, and was not helped by a lawyer who claimed to be ignorant. How could the system be challenged? If the Bibles had been the cause of the problem, perhaps this really was a religious issue.

Returning to the yacht, the Canadians again affirmed their allegiance: they would be standing with me all the way. I felt comforted by this, realizing that whilst I was the real target of the court, there would nevertheless be an implied acceptance of guilt if my friends were seen to run away. Although I did not mention this to them, it was a relief to have their commitment, and by implication, that of their Consul.

I could not stop thinking about the verbal charges thrown at us: we were subversives trying to overthrow the government. Yet here we were at large – free to roam the country! The irony of it all!

Early the following morning, Veikko and Matti told me that they wanted to return to Rabat to ask their Consul some more questions. Whilst this was a great surprise to me after the conversations of the previous night, I thought it was good to get more reassurance. Perhaps they could find out more about our case and what we could do. I offered to drive them to Rabat, but Matti declined, saying that they had talked and preferred to go by public transport. They packed their bags with what I thought was a lot of gear for a day-trip. I asked if they were planning to stay overnight.

'Well, you never know, we might get stuck there or do some sight-seeing, so it is better to be prepared,' Matti said nervously.

They did not return that night, or the following day. I became very anxious, but had no way of knowing where they might be or how to contact them, but convinced myself that they were enjoying the wonderful city of Rabat. I never saw them again.

It was several days later that I had a phone call from a distressed voice on a very bad line. It was Matti. He was crying and stuttering and my first concern was that he must be in trouble, either in Rabat or at the border. Had they tried to cross and been arrested, I wondered?

'Graham,' he blurted out, 'I am really so sorry, please forgive us.'

'Where are you, what is happening?' I asked.

'We are in Spain: at Malaga airport waiting for our flight to Canada that leaves soon. Please, please forgive us.'

I was almost lost for words. This was the last thing I expected.

I asked Matti what had happened to make them change their minds and, haltingly and hardly able to speak, he told me that on their last night on board the boat, they had talked and decided to change their minds and ask the Consul to help give them safe passage out of the country.

'It was too dangerous to stay,' he said. 'Our Consul was right. We had to get out. I will write when I get home to Canada.'

The phone went dead. I felt utterly abandoned.

That was the last I ever heard from either of my Finnish/Canadian friends.

I discovered later that they returned to Canada, but Matti never recovered from the grief or the guilt he felt from deserting me. A few months later I received an e-mail from a friend to tell me that he had committed suicide.

The following year I learned that Matti had many other personal problems that contributed to his death. I also learned that one of the reasons he wanted to come on this trip was to get away – to escape while he sorted out his life. He wanted his old friend Veikko with him, as he looked to him for spiritual guidance. He hoped to return from Morocco a new man, with a new business and a fresh start in life. I felt so sad, wondering how differently it could all have been if only he had parted with a packet of cigarettes on that first day, while he was enjoying the ride on my motor scooter. All this may have been avoided, I thought sorrowfully.

14. Awaiting the Appeal

Thursday 11th June

Now I was alone on the yacht. I often saw Jacques walking in the port, and he would come over for a chat, but he seemed distant. I tried on several occasions to find out why, but without success. Did he feel guilty because he had blamed me for the large books, the Study Bibles that had become an issue in the court? I did not want to make him feel bad about this. After all, I knew there was nothing illegal in those books, even if the authorities were not happy to see them in the country. I was prepared to fight for this principle, even if I did feel offended to learn that he had been advised not to admit that he brought them in. I did not blame him for taking the advice of his lawyer.

Jacques' camper van was parked outside his apartment. I was surprised it had not been moved by the customs officers who had custody of my motor-scooter. Jacques had even been able to travel around the country in the van, visiting friends on the coast over the weekend. I would have liked to use the scooter, which was far more pleasant in the heat than a car, but I did not like to ask for it in case it raised the question of Jacques' camper, and resulted in it too being confiscated.

Having discovered that my embassy was un-sympathetic and unhelpful, and that my lawyer could do little to defend me against the blatantly false charges, I was convinced that publicity was the only option. My plan was to find out as much as possible about the false accusations contained in the *Procès Verbal* and the court judgement, and then to present the injustice that had been done, in public. I was still in shock from the realization that there was no possibility of challenging those false charges at the appeal and was determined to fight back.

The friendly restaurant owners and their staff in the marina kept me informed about what the Moroccan press was reporting.

'Look, you are famous!' said one as he translated what had been written.

A front-page article included the accusation that I had several tons of Bibles on board.

'Where are they then?' I joked.

'They say you distributed them in the dead of night!' he replied.

I became angry just thinking about the stupidity of such a suggestion.

'Where did the information come from?' I asked.

He looked to the inside pages where the article was continued.

'Official sources … this is *your confession* to the court!'

I was constantly aware of my vulnerability. Small achievements meant a lot and helped keep at bay the depression and emotional turmoil I felt welling up on occasions. Even having access to the cheaper Spanish phone rates was a real bonus. Although the antenna I had rigged up on the yacht was excellent for computer com-munication to the internet via my mobile phone, I found normal speech reception was often poor in the marina.

By driving the short distance to a nearby beach not far from the border with Ceuta, I could obtain much clearer reception on the Spanish phone network.

My twenty-three-year-old son Mark came over from Spain for a few days, to keep me company and to look after the yacht while I was away in Tanger and elsewhere. I was still afraid that if the yacht was unattended, the customs authorities might make a move to confiscate it. I was becoming bolder, and felt more secure as the days went by. Whenever possible I became more assertive, pressing to see how far I could go. At all costs I had to make the authorities respect me. It was perhaps the only way to preserve my dignity and avoid collapsing under the constant pressure.

One afternoon a marina worker came over and told me that the yacht had to be moved.

'Over to the far side of the port,' he said, pointing towards the customs office.

'I don't want to move, I am very happy here,' I said, 'but I'll talk to the Marina Director.'

I suspected this was another crude attempt by the customs to gain possession, but thought I could override the order, as the director was ultimately responsible for berth allocations. I walked over to discuss the move.

Unfortunately, when I arrived at the office he was absent. The receptionist there, who spoke perfect English, informed me that a large ferry-boat would arrive later in the day, requiring the space where I was moored.

'You have to move your boat,' she insisted, pointing to the area outside her office.

'But I am the only visitor in the marina,' I said. 'The ferry can go anywhere!'

'No, it has to go over there, she insisted.'

I knew very well where the ferry went, and also knew that its service from Spain did not begin until August.

'All right, I will move for the ferry,' I said, 'but I want to go to the jetty at right angles to the one I am on.'

It was only twenty metres away from where I was now.

She objected to this idea and again told me I had to move where she directed. I then demanded to know the real reason I was being ordered to move. I informed her that I knew there was no ferry due until August. She was either too embarrassed or proud to tell me the truth: that she had been told by the customs officers to move me nearer to their facilities. Finally I told her that I would talk to the director on his return.

Arriving back at the yacht, I discussed a plan with Mark to use a long rope at the bow and stern. After

Police and one of the ever-present 'watchers' in Marina Smir.

releasing the securing lines, we would walk the yacht the short distance to my preferred new position, without starting the engine. Suspecting that this would cause a stir, we prepared the ropes and waited until no one was near the yacht, then quickly released the lines. I jumped off, leaving Mark to pull on the long bowline, while I pulled the stern around towards the new place. There was no wind to assist or oppose us, and it took several seconds for the twenty-ton vessel to gain momentum. Slowly she began to creep away from the jetty, under our control.

Within two minutes, the anticipated commotion began. Several whistles shrilled and police car sirens sounded. More worrying was the reaction of the warship moored on the other side of the marina. Its engine started with a roar like distant thunder, and a cloud of blue smoke belched out of the stern, enveloping it. Officers came running from all directions towards us. I heard another familiar sound: Mohammed's black Ford Capri was again on the move, roaring around the marina with tyres screeching, heading in our direction. I was nervous but knew we had no option but to continue the manoeuvre.

'Dad, Dad, what shall we do?' Mark shouted.

'Take no notice and keep pulling,' I told him.

We were almost at the new position, now only sixty feet away. The chief customs officer arrived right behind me, and began shouting in Arabic.

Someone screamed in English: 'Stop, Stop!'

I momentarily let the line slack and pointed to the yacht, which continued its momentum and told him not to be so stupid. Another officer drew his pistol and waved it wildly, pointing it in my direction. I turned and laughingly raised one hand in a mocking 'hands up' gesture, while heaving with all my weight on the rope with the other. We were almost at the correct angle to the jetty and nearing our new berth. I quickly secured the bow rope onto the large iron bollard on the pontoon, and jumped onto the foredeck, running aft to assist Mark pull in the stern line and secure it.

The whole manoeuvre took less than five minutes. We were suddenly aware that the commotion had stopped, apart from the deep throbbing of the gunboat engine. We looked at each other and laughed heartily as we adjusted the ropes, making the yacht secure in her new position.

Looking around, we saw the crowd of officers huddled on the jetty arguing with each other. Some were already sauntering off. A marina worker came cycling up and asked in Spanish why we had moved, since permission was needed. I told him that far from needing permission, I had been ordered by his colleague to move, as a ferry would be arriving.

'What ferry?' he asked.

I just stared after him as he cycled off saying: *'Bien! Bien!'*

Within a few minutes, all the officers had wandered away and the gunboat engine was again silent. My adrenaline rush subsided as we went below for a celebratory cup of tea. Once again, I felt a small victory had been gained over 'the enemy' – the authorities, and perhaps more importantly my own fear.

Later that day, I returned to visit the marina reception area. This office, together with those of the police and customs, were all located in the same large building at the entrance to the port. We had tied the yacht alongside here on our arrival, to complete customs and immigration formalities. Each department had its own separate access pathway leading to its facilities. As usual, I took a short cut along the path leading to the police station, and then walked across the grass to the marina office. Several officers were sitting outside under the shade of a tree, as always. I passed them with the usual greeting: '*Salam Alikhum.*' They all looked at me, but there was no response as I carried on past. This was most unusual. Arabs are always courteous, even to their enemies!

Once inside the marina office, I informed the receptionist that I had moved the yacht. She chuckled approvingly with a wink, but said nothing. Walking out, I decided to return along the same path, again greeting the officers.

As I was just past them, Mohammed shouted from his office door: 'Graham, Graham!'

I turned as he questioned, 'Why did you move your yacht?'

I answered, 'I like this new position; it is quieter. Anyway,' I joked, 'I had so much fun moving and seeing your officers running around waving their guns and blowing whistles, that I was thinking of making another move tomorrow, just to give them more excitement and much-needed exercise!'

Mohammed laughed and said, 'You know, Graham, if you move your yacht a little each day within a week you could be home in Spain!'

I roared with laughter, along with the other officers who all stood up and shook my hand. Another breakthrough, I thought, as I bounced back to the yacht feeling elated.

Several days passed as I waited for the date of the appeal to be set. Some friends came to visit from Spain and while we were eating in one of the marina restaurants, my phone rang. It was the British Vice Consul in Rabat.

'What was the outcome of the court appeal this morning?' she enquired.

Surprised and not understanding the question, I asked her to repeat it.

'There has been no appeal yet, as far as I know,' I told her.

'I thought as much,' she said gruffly. 'There was an appeal scheduled for today, several hours ago, but I have only just been informed of this by the Ministry of Justice. Your lawyer was also not informed; I checked.'

My lawyer phoned later in the day to tell me that indeed an appeal had been scheduled, but that since no one had appeared in court, it had been postponed. The court later insisted that all parties had been informed. The Justice Ministry gave a different story to the embassy, explaining that we were not informed because no one knew of my whereabouts, believing me to be in England, since that was my home country.

While awaiting the appeal, I had a call on my mobile from CNN in the United States, asking if they could interview me about the case. I was delighted, though rather nervous. I was asked to be available at nine o'clock in the evening, Moroccan time. It was going to be a live broadcast. Shortly before the appointed time I drove close to Ceuta, as usual, in order to guarantee a good signal on the Spanish mobile phone network, parking near the beach in readiness for the call.

At exactly nine o'clock the phone rang.

'Is that Doctor Hutt? Are you ready for the interview?'

'Yes, I am ready!'

First the interviewer gave an on-air report of my situation and then asked, 'What were the charges against you?'

'As far as I know,' I told him, 'we are charged with a minor customs violation: that of not paying duty on some Bibles. But since there is no duty on books here, and since these are not forbidden in Morocco, I am confused!'

'What about the fines: 42,000 Dollars; wasn't it and is it true you have a prison sentence too?' he asked.

'Yes, it is true,' I answered. 'We assume more is involved than we have yet discovered.'

I was standing outside the car as we were talking, when someone came up to me and began tapping on the phone, gesticulating me to stop the call.

Thinking it was probably a police informer, I said, 'I'm sorry, someone is trying to get me to stop the interview: I may have to go.'

Then an idea came to me. I reached into my pocket and pulled out the first Dirham note I came across and handed it to him. He scuttled away, much to my relief. I had no idea how much I gave him.

'Are there any religious implications?' I was asked.

'Not as far as I know, except that Bibles were the subject of the case. But the Moroccan press has been reporting this as a religious matter: nothing less than an attempt to overthrow Islam! I am still waiting for a translation of local newspaper reports that several workers in the marina have told me about.'

The interviewer asked, 'Was there any suggestion of proselytising?'

I told him that our only contact with Moroccans prior to the case had been with port officials, police and customs officers. There was no suggestion, I said with a laugh, of our being accused of trying to convert them – at least as far as I knew.

'How were you treated while in custody?'

I expressed my disgust at not being allowed an interpreter during the long interviews. Nor were we given a translation of what we later found out was a police report, full of false statements and accusations. I reiterated my other complaints and said that in all probability we would still have been in a cell had I not been able to make a secret call from my mobile phone whilst in the toilet of the police interrogation centre.

I was asked more about the penalties imposed: the fine, jail sentence, and confiscation of my yacht.

'It all sounds a very high price to pay, whatever you did, doesn't it?' he asked.

'Yes, it is still something of a mystery at this point,' I told him. 'A diplomat has informed me that there are other hidden, "verbal charges" but it is difficult to know exactly what these are. Oh, and one of the official charges is of illegal entry and avoiding customs checks, both of which are false accusations – and I can prove it: I have an entry stamp in my passport and the stamped customs declaration!'

The interview lasted for about fifteen minutes, going into further details about the conditions during our detention.

'Will there be an opportunity to speak on further occasions?' he asked. 'We would like to follow the case.'

I agreed to this before disconnecting and making extensive notes of the conversation before driving off.

Another interview with CNN took place the following day. I listened as the reporter explained to viewers about the case and updated them on yesterday's conversation. He then announced that he had talked with the Moroccan Embassy in Washington a few hours ago. The CNN staff had subsequently been informed in a fax that my case concerned a charge of a minor nature: that of not completing the correct customs declaration, and thus avoiding a small amount of duty on some books.

'Can you explain how the sentencing came to be so absurdly harsh for such a minor offence?' he asked.

'Sorry, but you have more information than I do,' I told him. 'I can only repeat that there is obviously a hidden agenda about which we know little, as yet. Moroccan press reports tell a very different story from that coming from the embassy officials.'

'I can't tell you how distressing it is to find that most of my information so far has come not from my lawyer or from the embassy, but from waiters and police in the marina who read the press reports on my case. And from a kind consular official of a different embassy than my own, who officially should not have told me anything!'

He asked how the British Embassy was assisting. I laughed and told him that when I spoke with the Vice Consul at the British Embassy in Rabat, she had discouraged me from even visiting!

Again, as soon as the interview was over and before returning to the yacht, I wrote down everything I could remember of the interview in order to later compile a log of events and conversations. I really hoped that this international coverage would somehow draw out the truth regarding the charges against me, forcing officials to examine the case.

Phone point on the beach. Overlooking the Spanish enclave or Ceuta where the phone interviews took place.

15. The *Procès Verbal*

Friday 12 June

When I arrived at the Tetouan court to meet my lawyer as arranged, I was finally handed a copy of the long-requested *Procès Verbal*. Although the form was headed in French, the text was in the now familiar, faint-typed Arabic, and was unintelligible to me. I asked for the phone number and address of the court interpreter who could translate the document for me. Abdullah seemed reluctant to provide this.

'You don't need a translation,' he exclaimed. 'The document is irrelevant to the case, and cannot be used as evidence in the court.'

I protested that as far as I understood from Moroccan press reports, it had already been extensively used against me. Furthermore the level of the fine indicated this.

'Anyway, Abdullah, how can you say it was not relevant or used, when the judge was reading from it in court?' I said.

With a sigh, he finally gave me the number of Adil, the same translator whom the judge would not allow to interpret for me in the court. I immediately phoned his office in Tanger from outside the court, hoping I could take the documents to him immediately. Tetouan was well on the way to Tanger. Adil agreed, and said that he could begin work on the document that same afternoon.

The roads were clear as I made the journey once again over the top of the Rif Mountains and descended into the Bay of Tanger. I soon found his office on the outskirts of the city. Once inside, he ordered coffee and we briefly discussed the case. He again apologized that he was not permitted to interpret for us in court and said that this was unusual.

We discussed the document I wanted translated and to my great surprise, learned that he already had copies. Adil admitted they were not official court documents but would not tell me how or why he obtained them. I assumed that it was through the lawyer, but later discovered that this was not so.

Since Adil had such an interest in the case and was present in the court, presumably understanding everything that went on, I asked him to explain what had transpired during the proceedings, hoping to find out more than my lawyer would divulge. He could not shed any light on the nature of the charges and explained that the judges had spoken so softly that it was impossible to hear what was said, even though he was standing just behind me. He knew from reading the newspapers, however, that I would find everything in the *Procès Verbal*.

'This is the case,' he said, holding up the papers. 'This is what the court has released to the media.'

Leaving my copies with him I returned to the marina via Tetouan and M'Diq, with a feeling of great anticipation and even excitement at the prospect of receiving the completed translation. Adil seemed a very affable and intelligent young man. His English was excellent and I felt I could trust him.

It took several days for the documents to be translated, but finally Adil phoned me at the marina, and offered to bring the finished documents. He quoted a price, which I thought was very high, but he said this was an official translation, authenticated with a seal.

I waited on deck in the setting sun for Adil to arrive. There were very few people around, apart from the usual policemen slowly pacing up and down. Then I saw a car drive down the short road leading into the port. As it arrived, several police officers seemed to appear from nowhere and surround the car, which I then recognized was a taxi. I could see from this distance that a conversation was in progress with two of the officers leaning into the front windows on either side.

My translator, dressed in a smart suit and tie, got out of the taxi and approached the yacht. Being the only yacht in the port, it was not difficult for him to find me. I beckoned him to come on board; he declined. As I jumped off and shook his hand, I noticed he was trembling, sweating, and very pale. I asked what was wrong and he reported that the police had apprehended him on arrival. They had informed him of exactly what time he had departed by bus from Tanger and when he hailed a taxi from the bus depot in M'Diq, and that they knew all his movements. Clearly, he was extremely shaken at the level of surveillance on his activities. They also demanded a copy of the documents he was carrying, but he told them they would have to ask me for these.

I pointed out that there were over fifty police in this port, and that they knew everything that was going on.

'This is the best evidence that the charges against me are false,' I told him. 'They know exactly how we arrived, who came and what has gone from my yacht: nothing like what has been reported in the Moroccan press.'

As I was about to pay Adil, he asked if I wanted copies of the other defendants' *Procès Verbals*, as well as mine.

'Yes, they would be useful,' I answered, concealing my surprise that he also had these.

I wondered if he knew that they had already departed for Spain. He drew out a thick envelope of papers from his leather briefcase and handed them to me. I counted out the cash and paid him before he rushed off to the waiting taxi.

Once again I felt elated, anticipating the pleasure of learning at last what our case was based on. I hurried down below deck and opened the large white envelope, laying the pages out on the table.

The document was headed in capitals:

KINGDOM OF MOROCCO: MINISTRY OF THE INTERIOR. GENERAL DIRECTOR OF NATIONAL SECURITY. REGION SECURITY OF TETOUAN: *PROCÈS VERBAL.*

It continued:

On June 1st 1998 at 10:00, Yasini Zouaoui, police officer, head of the third judicial section of the Regional Department of Tetouan: by virtue of flagrante-delicto and in accordance with the nature of the case and by the assistance of the police inspector of this section …

On the grounds of the report submitted by the commissariat of M'Diq under No. 8785 dated May 31st 1998 … concerning Hutt Graham, born in 1994 at Caversham, retired and residing at 10 Totland …

There were three erroneous statements in the first few lines: my date of birth made me four years old; the address was incorrect, as was my occupation. I read on with interest. It became obvious that there was almost nothing correct in the report. My education was totally invented, including the universities I had attended, none of which I had mentioned. It stated that: 'I am working for three companies – in Lebanon, South Holland and England – charged with editing the books I had brought in [Arabic Bibles] and responsible for distribution.'

All was written in the first person. This was my confession. It claimed that I had signed the document, and that an English translation accompanied it. This was far worse than I had anticipated. Did the court really believe all of this? It went on to state that I brought with me: 'Twenty-three tons of "Studied New Testaments" along with other books.' There was a list of several countries I had visited in order 'to distribute the books for the purpose of persuading poor weak-minded Muslims to convert to Christianity'.

As I read through the countries, I remembered volunteering to the officer, during the interrogation, some of the places I had visited over the past thirty years. These were the countries, in the precise order I had listed them.

In the 'Summing Up' towards the end of the document, it stated: 'It was proved that the persons involved in this case came to Morocco with the common purpose and intent of distributing the books in order that Moroccans would embrace Christianity: to shake the Islamic faith, taking advantage of the great needs of the victims.'

Here was the reality, at last. In spite of what I had been told by British Embassy officials and by my lawyer, there was an implication – indeed a supposed confession of a religious nature – of proselytising. This was the first concrete evidence I had for this.

Everything was now falling into place. There was nothing illegal in bringing Bibles to Morocco, but it *was* an offence to proselytise, even though, as I discovered later, this was a guaranteed human right, according to treaties signed by the government. The document also supported the claim made by the Canadian Consul that I was charged with trying to overthrow the Islamic government. Subversion was implied by the statement that we 'had come together as a group, plotting to convert feeble-minded Muslims'.

The document finished by stating that the whole document was 'read to the defendant in English, before he signed it in the presence of the Assistant'.

I found it difficult to believe the falsehood of this statement, and had to read it twice. Not only was it not signed; it certainly was not read to me, in any language. Reading through the other *Procès Verbals*, which the translator had provided me with for Matti, Veikko, Jacques and Françoise, there was little apparent difference, except that it was implied in their statements that they were all working for me. The only relief was that I was beginning to understand what was going on. It was all the more alarming though that there seemed no legal way, according to the lawyer, to challenge these false statements.

It took two hours to read carefully through all the documents again, before I sat back, and tried to summarize them in my mind. I then phoned Abdullah and told him that I had a translation of the documents and was amazed at their contents.

He sounded irritated and told me, 'So what? It is of no consequence it was not allowed to be used in court.'

I repeated that the Moroccan press was quoting the exact words of this document, and claimed to have got the information from 'official sources at the court'.

'How can you tell me it was not used in court?' I retorted angrily.

'Do you realize that I was accused of bringing in twenty-three *tons* of books?'

'Yes, I know, but no one believed that!' he said.

I then insisted on having a copy of the judgement so that I could see for myself if this document had been used as evidence.

'Oh, that will take a long time,' he told me dismissively. 'Some weeks at least.'

Just how practical would it be to change lawyers? I wondered. I was aware by now that the function of Moroccan lawyers was to represent their client, rather than defend them. Having contacted the British Embassy I was assured that Mr Abdullah was one of the most experienced lawyers in Morocco. It was quite worrying to know that although he would be my legal representative, there were defined limits as to what he could do to present a real defence at the appeal. Even on his own admission, he could not challenge false accusations or judgements of the court.

Later that evening, I phoned the translator and thanked him for his work and explained that I now needed a copy of the court judgement as well. I asked if he could obtain this document and translate it for me. He said that it was possible, and quoted a price. I would soon be in a position to compare the two documents, and hopefully prove beyond doubt that the *Procès Verbal* had been used – illegally – in court.

Later I discovered that it was not only illegal to use an unsigned document, but equally illegal to present a document that was self-incriminating, even if it was signed. I was informed that any document produced by a defendant that incriminated himself could not be used in a court of law. On so many counts, it was now apparent that the court had acted unjustly.

Taking a break from the intensity of studying the documents, I went to visit my Moroccan friend at his nearby restaurant. We were chatting over tea in the mid-June sun when another friend from Ceuta arrived. He brought with him a copy of one of the local newspapers, *Al Jaser.* It contained an article about my case, along with a translation into English. The article read:

> June 14th 1998, quoting from Moroccan sources: On May 29th a boat was searched and nothing illegal was found. However, doubts about the intention of the owner, caused the police to put the boat under surveillance. Guards saw a man moving goods from the yacht to apartment No. 46, belonging to Jacques Delors and his wife by motor scooter. The police checked the apartment and found a quantity of books which they confiscated.

It continued:

> Three men were accused by the court and confessed that they were serving organizations for the purpose of propaganda and brought into Morocco materials and books for seducing people, and for the purpose of weakening and shaking the Islamic faith in our country. The British man stated in court that he had mounted such operations in many other countries, including Tunisia, Libya, Syria, Egypt, Turkey, Malta, Lebanon, Kuwait, Dubai, Abu Dhabi and Qatar.
>
> He further stated in court that he had never visited Morocco before and took this opportunity in the dead of night to distribute this Catholic literature. The other defendants admitted that they came to Marina Smir to assist in saturating Morocco with these materials. The Frenchman confessed that he agreed to store the books. He declared through his lawyer, Locous, that he had no responsibility for importing the books and had no connection with the case, except for storing the goods.

The prosecutor requested a fine of 500 Dirhams for each person and a prison sentence of two months. The four were found guilty of all these admitted crimes and the court sentenced them to a fine of 420,000 Dirhams, a prison sentence of two months and confiscation of the yacht, motor scooter and the camper van-trailer in which was discovered more books.

It was immediately obvious that far from being irrelevant, the *Procès Verbal* was the single most damaging document on which the whole case rested. It said that we were guilty of the stated crimes, and that we had signed our acceptance of guilt having read and understood the statement. Yet we could do nothing to correct these lies. I never did discover why the sentence was so much heavier than that requested by the King's Prosecutor on behalf of the customs authorities. This was 'unheard of' according to Abdullah.

I could not help considering Jacques' actions while we were in police custody. Did he know what was going on when he pressured the others to sign the document? Was he aware, all along, that the blame would eventually be placed on me? He was able to converse with the officers and perhaps was persuaded that this was the best course of action, at least for himself and his wife.

I decided to wait for an appropriate time to challenge Jacques on the contents of the press report: to ask him about the other books and, most important, his denial of bringing the Bibles into the country. If I could persuade him to admit to bringing them in, it could have a beneficial impact at the appeal. I could see no disadvantage whatsoever if he admitted that he drove into Morocco with the books, clearing customs in Ceuta. He had carried nothing illegal.

16. The Final Desertion

Saturday 13th June

Weeks had passed since the trial, yet no date had been set for the appeal. Members of my family and friends came over regularly to assist me in 'holding out' on the yacht. This enabled me to relax while travelling, especially when I needed to visit Tanger or elsewhere. I felt secure in the port since moving the boat the short distance in the marina. From this position we could see the approach of any unwelcome visitors.

One morning, as I was walking in the port I met Mohammed together with his deputy. He was unusually friendly and invited me for tea in the nearby café. He asked casually how things were going and what was happening about the appeal.

'I know that you have friends in the government. Are they helping you?'

Before I was able to answer, he volunteered, 'You know, the real problem is those large "Study Bibles" that Jacques had in his apartment.'

I told him I had nothing to do with those; Jacques had purchased them in Ceuta quite legally. Mohammed smiled and said, 'Yes, I know: we know everything you have on the yacht and what came off it!'

'OK Mohammed,' I said. 'So what? If this is a simple case of avoidance of duty on books, why were the penalties so high, and what is the significance of those few copies of a Study Bible?'

'These books were different. The judge said they were for converting Muslims,' he said.

'But we had not spoken with any Moroccans during the few hours between our arrival and arrest!'

He said nothing and continued sipping, straining the green mint leaves through his teeth.

I went on to express how unhappy I was that we had no idea of what actually happened in the court, and knew nothing about the supposed 'confessions' that we were alleged to have made to the police.

'This is not a police matter. As far as we are concerned, the case is closed. It is entirely a matter for the *Douane*[1] as no laws have been broken,' he affirmed.

'But it was you who arrested us!' I protested.

'Yes, we had to check to see what was in that bag,' he said, sounding almost apologetic.

If that was the case, it now seemed that the whole incident was contrived. Could it be that they were looking for something – anything – that would give them an excuse to take the yacht? I now remembered a waiter informing me that there was someone interested in my yacht and realized that perhaps this was the missing link.

'Use your contacts,' Mohammed advised. 'The longer this goes on, the more difficult it will be to get your boat back.'

With that, he abruptly stood up. As he departed, he said, 'If you ever want to bring anything to the port, you only have to ask me and I will help.'

---

[1] The customs authorities.

Wishing me luck, and placing his hand on my shoulder, he returned to his office. I felt this was a genuine offer.

At the same time I was confused by what Mohammed had said and was still left with many questions. Had he not got me into this situation, as an act of revenge for the photograph incident, a year or more ago? I remembered his anger when he returned with the black prints the day after the incident. He accused me of tricking him since they were all blank. He knew that I had swapped the film.

Was he genuinely sorry that this incident had led to so much trouble as he indicated? I believed he was. How was I to deal with the fact that it now seemed to be the contents of one particular book – one that I had nothing to do with – which was the problem? If it was a customs offence and was now nothing to do with the police, then why was this an issue? There was also the charge of illegal entry that he had not mentioned. Many things made little sense. I found it impossible to feel angry towards Mohammed and felt that he was sincerely trying to help me now, even if he had initiated the incident.

It was not difficult to see why there was such a desire, in a restrictive country, to obtain a copy of the Bible. It is always the things that are unavailable that are most attractive, especially to enquiring minds. I could see, too, why the Study Bibles, with their helpful notes and explanations of the text, history and context, were considered dangerous. The stupidity of this case remained: according to the law, the books were all legal, including those Jacques had brought from Ceuta. No one had been able to find any law that made Bibles illegal in the country. There simply was no case to answer. Even the suggestion that customs duties were avoided was false: there was no duty on books.

It was time to visit Jacques and try to find out if the news report in *Al Jaser*, regarding his Study Bibles, was correct. He was friendly and invited me into his apartment for coffee. Communication was not easy. I struggled to convey my concern that, although I had been happy to take responsibility for the problems in general, I had no knowledge of the other books. I told him of my talk with Mohammed, and how it now transpired that in some way, these few copies of Study Bibles were the real problem, according to the police.

Jacques eventually admitted that his lawyer had insisted that his defence should be to claim that he took no part in bringing in any book. 'Insist that they all came from the yacht,' he was advised to say.

'But the port police know this is false,' I told him. 'They know there is no way I could have unloaded those books, still in their cartons, right under their noses.'

Jacques was not prepared to discuss this any further and terminated the conversation.

As I wandered around the port the next day, I noticed Jacques' camper van was missing from its usual parking place outside his apartment. I walked over to the customs office to see if it had been moved there, thinking the officers may have carried out the confiscation order. After all, they had locked away my motor-scooter since the night of the arrest. The van was nowhere to be seen.

The following day my friend Juan from Algeciras phoned.

'Jacques is OK,' he said. 'He is here with us.'

I was shocked. Obviously detecting this from my silence he explained, 'But you discussed this, no? Didn't you both agree that this was the best thing to do?'

I sighed resignedly and said, 'We have not even discussed it since the day after the trial, at which time Jacques pledged his support for me, insisting that he would stay to the end of the appeal process, however long it took. He even reaffirmed this commitment the day Veikko and Matti left.'

For some time after Jacques' departure, I felt devastated. Even though we had difficulty in communicating, at least he was a familiar face, a comfort to have nearby and a moral support. After all, he too was at least as implicated as I was. To be left to fight on alone worried me. Until now, I had also felt the comfort and security of having another embassy involved in the case. I knew that the French, like the Canadian Embassy staff, would not allow their citizens to be abused. I did not have any such confidence in my embassy.

Once again, I began to wonder at the implications. All those who had signed the *Procès Verbal* had now left the country. Did that make me more vulnerable, or less? Would the authorities now feel obliged to arrest and imprison me, in order to get the fine paid? How would I raise $42,000 to get out of prison, if they applied the court ruling? Or perhaps the opposite would be true. Since I was the only one who did not sign, and had made no attempt to leave the country, perhaps the authorities would be more inclined to accept my innocence and find it easier now to simply let me go?

If I could obtain a statement from Jacques about those Study Bibles, now that he was safely in Spain, would it help? Either way, if the judgement could not be contested, how could I ever get my yacht returned? I felt really confused and depressed, not knowing whom to turn to for advice.

I felt some admiration for Jacques: that he dared – and had succeeded – to leave Morocco with his camper van, which had been confiscated by the court along with my yacht. I knew it was impossible to pass through the border without declaring the vehicle. All details are entered into the computer there. As soon as he went through passport control on leaving the country, it would be evident that he had entered with that vehicle. Surely the court would have informed the Ministry of the Interior that the vehicle was now in the custody of the customs authorities? Was this yet further evidence that the court had no intention of applying the penalties to the others, but was happy and relieved to see them depart, leaving me on my own? It was all a great worry. I learned later that it was his Consul who had urged him to leave while he had the opportunity.

I received an e-mail from one of my American friends working in the Senate, advising me that there was a huge press campaign going on in the United States in my support; I was to expect calls from more television and radio stations who were following the case. It was seen in America as an issue of blatant religious persecution. 'You should ask your embassy to assist in securing your yacht until the appeal, in case the customs authorities try to sell it before the judicial process is completed,' she wrote. 'The embassy staff will know of this procedure and help.'

I decided to visit the British Embassy in Rabat and phoned to make an appointment to see the Consular officials. Again I was discouraged from visiting.

'You should go to the Consul in Tanger if you need anything,' I was curtly informed, 'but come if you must!'

This time I insisted.

The previous evening, my eldest daughter Ruth had arrived from England to keep me company for ten days, while she revised for her medical exams. I left her with the yacht – sure of her competence to deal with any officials or trouble while I was away. As I set off on the four-hour journey to Rabat, I felt more secure because I had managed to procure a second mobile phone. I could be in constant communication with whoever was on the yacht, even while I was travelling.

It was Tuesday 16th June when I set out on the road to Rabat. As I drove, a friend from England phoned to tell me that he had contacted the Moroccan Embassy in London. An official there had informed him that the charges 'were of a very minor nature involving the avoidance of fifty pounds in customs duty on some books'. He had asked the official to explain why the penalties were so high for such a minor offence, and was told that this was 'being investigated', as there was 'some confusion'. Despite many further requests, both from individuals and from eminent members of the British Parliament, the Moroccan authorities never came up with an explanation.

On my arrival at the British Embassy I was shown into the office of the Vice Consul. She began by quizzing me about the two people in Morocco whose names I had given her colleague, the Consul in Tanger, to phone on my behalf. Whilst I felt angry at this intrusion, I explained that both connections were linked to the book I was writing on North Africa. I explained that one of these people had set up contacts for me with government officials, and the other was very knowledge-able about Asilah: one of the ports about which I was writing.

Then I asked, 'Why are you interrogating me about my contacts: surely I have the right to have friends in Morocco?'

'We consider this curious, since this is your first visit to Morocco,' she responded.

'Why do you insist this is my first visit? I have actually visited hundreds of times, and have a letter from the Ministry of the Interior regarding my work here,' I told her.

She was not interested in looking at the letter, which was pinned inside my passport, but she did become a little calmer and more civil towards me, seemingly satisfied with my explanation that she admitted explained 'some things'.

We then discussed the *Procès Verbal.* The Vice Consul insisted, 'The court has rejected the contents of this. In any case, it cannot be legally used as evidence because you did not sign it. And, it is known to contain erroneous information.'

I was surprised at how much she knew about it. I informed her that I was sure it had been used: a fact, I informed her, confirmed by the Canadian Consul to her nationals.

The official then launched into an acrimonious conversation about Bibles in Morocco. It was illegal to have these in the country, she said. I insisted that there was nothing illegal about them and that, furthermore, even Mohammed, the Prophet of Islam, had encouraged his followers to read the Christian Scriptures. She scoffed at this and countered that we had acted unlawfully, and that the penalties received were entirely reasonable in any Muslim country.

I was furious to hear this misinformation from my Consul. Even the police did not believe any crime had been committed and were emphatic that there was no longer any police involvement. It was purely a matter for the customs authorities. She disagreed vehemently with this. I added that the King's Prosecutor had said exactly the same thing initially, telling us that we would only have to pay ten Dollars to the customs authorities for failing to fill out a form declaring everything on the yacht.

The Vice Consul then talked about Christian activity in Spain, where Bibles are offered as gifts to anyone travelling from Spain to North Africa by ferry.

I knew about this, and had been offered an Arabic New Testament myself when crossing by car the previous year. But, I asked her: 'What has that got to do with my case? It is perfectly legal in Spain to give and to receive a Bible – Spain is part of Europe!'

I asked her to explain why she was inferring that the case was related to the illegality of Bibles in a Muslim country, yet also insisted it was a secular case of avoiding duty on books. Either it was a religious issue or a customs offence. 'Or was it both?' I asked. She abruptly closed this subject.

I felt increasingly alarmed at the thought that I was also on trial at the British Embassy. I had come looking for support, help and advice, not for a cross-examination. Why all these questions? I was supposed to be convicted of a customs offence, according to the Consul, yet the implication from her questioning was that there was far more to the case. The Vice Consul seemed no less officious than the interrogators in Tetouan police headquarters!

I then discussed with her my dissatisfaction with the way in which we had been treated by the police during the initial interrogation, especially since we were told a deliberate lie, and since we were coerced into signing documents having been told that this would enable our immediate release, whereas in truth, these were designed to ensure we would be imprisoned.

She angrily countered again that the *Procès Verbal* was irrelevant, since it could not be used as evidence in court. Again I pointed out that it had. It was the principal document on the judge's bench during the trial and had been handed to the local press as my 'confession' before I had even known its contents.

'Impossible!' she growled vehemently.

Before leaving, another official agreed to submit a formal complaint to the appropriate authorities concerning our treatment while in detention; particularly the fact that the British Embassy had not been informed by the police of my detention and that we were neither fed nor allowed water.

It was obvious that I would get no further assistance here and I returned to the marina disheartened, wondering if, after all, I should have heeded the advice of the official who had tried to dissuade me from visiting in the first place.

17. Upping the Stakes

Wednesday 17th June

I decided to do everything I could to prepare for my own defence prior to the appeal, the date for which was still awaited. There were only two practical options open to me: I could increase the publicity in order to demonstrate that the accusations against me were false or I could call on my Moroccan friends for help, something I had been reluctant to do until now. I knew that none of my friends would mind trying to help. On the contrary, they would be offended if I did not call on their assistance.

Both options were risky. Further publicity might inflame the authorities and make things worse. I had been warned by my embassy that the publicity could only have negative consequences. If my high-ranking friends could not help, then I had no further way out.

I was concerned that the police or some other authority would create a situation that would result in my arrest and imprisonment on the grounds of infringement of the bail conditions – if there were any. I had heard that it was common for police to plant drugs or stolen goods on people in order to obtain a conviction. This was not unknown even in England and the United States, so why would it be any less likely in Morocco? I recalled the warning given by the Canadian Consul, to be careful when I travelled.

One of my friends, Hassan, lived in Casablanca. I called him and explained my difficulties. After I had listed the penalties imposed by the court, there was a long silence.

'There must be more to the case: were arms involved ... or drugs?'

I was astonished. 'Come on Hassan, you know me better than that!'

'Yes, I am sorry,' he apologized, 'but no court would convict anyone for bringing in books, even if they were Bibles. I have never heard of such fines and penalties being imposed for anything short of arms trafficking or major offences. Even drug smugglers do not get such penalties' he said.

Laughingly, he then asked if I was familiar with the smuggling that went on across the border every day just a few miles away.

'Oh yes, I know all about that!' I affirmed. It was somewhat of a relief that he found my situation so bizarre. He offered to look into it, and to contact his friend at the Justice Ministry.

'If it is only books involved,' he promised, 'I can be sure to get the case resolved for you.'

Over the coming days I contacted other friends and told them of my problem. Some had heard or read of the case in the press. All were sympathetic and said that they would do everything they could to help.

A return e-mail from across the Atlantic told me that several Senators and Congressmen had been informed about my plight and wanted to take up the issue as a fundamental breach of human and religious rights, in contravention of international agreements. I was asked if

I was prepared for press coverage to increase. I replied that I saw no other option, but explained that my embassy had advised against it.

I received information by e-mail from other friends monitoring the situation in Washington, telling me that following my interviews with CNN, many people had been making enquiries at the Moroccan Embassy there. These resulted in two completely different stories being told. One Senator, when asking about my case, was informed that the arrest was for a minor customs offence, as reported by CNN. Another was told that the case involved much more serious charges of sedition. When the Senators compared notes and queried the reason for two different stories, they were asked to 'await clarification'. It was comforting to know that even Moroccan officials were confused. I knew that the level of publicity and the reported confusion must eventually get to the ears of higher officials who I hoped would intervene.

Weeks dragged on while I awaited the date of an appeal. There was no news from Hassan and I was reluctant to hassle him but I eventually phoned his office.

'I'm really sorry,' he said. 'There is nothing I can do to help. I have been ordered not to get involved. My contact in the Justice Ministry told me that you were detained on very serious charges, including smuggling and distributing seventeen tons of Bibles.'

'Do you believe that?' I asked.

Hassan went on to tell me that he had also been informed of other, more serious charges, including illegal entry into Morocco. I could hear from his tone of voice that he doubted the information, but I also realized that he was powerless to help further. Again he apologized and asked me to put my case in writing and fax it to him, and he would make a direct appeal to another friend – this time in the palace. I realized that the answer he had been given was simply to ensure that he would not get involved. I greatly appreciated his promise to press further, knowing the risk he was taking on my behalf.

More calls to Abdullah brought forth the same response as before: 'Don't worry, this is a minor case, everything will be overturned at the appeal ...' etc. He went on to say that there were many irregularities in this case, and many legal points that he would be presenting to ensure dismissal of the case. I told him that I had heard all this from him before the first trial, and had no confidence in his ability to defend me any better at the appeal.

I mentioned my concern that the Moroccan Embassy in Washington and others were still quoting from the *Procès Verbal,* and presenting this as my 'confession'.

'You told me that this report was rejected before the court even sat.'

He sounded offended but agreed. Again he told me not to worry: 'Trust me!'

He knew that I had diplomatic friends in the United States and asked if it was possible for me to obtain help from the American Embassy in Rabat. He said that based on his experience, officials there would be far more helpful. I replied that I was working on it, and asked if it would be acceptable to get an outside international lawyer to attend the appeal, both to monitor the hearing and to assist him. Christian Solidarity Worldwide had heard about the case and recently corresponded: they offered to provide a lawyer. He agreed that this would be a good idea, but said the law dictated that only a Moroccan, registered to practice law in the country, could represent the accused in court.

Further news from across the Atlantic revealed that the story emerging from the Moroccan authorities had been clarified. It no longer mentioned the minor customs offence. When the embassy was asked about the case, the faxed response to one Senator, copied to me via e-mail, read:

> Dr Hutt and his friends admitted the charges of bringing into Morocco books and other literature, which they intended to distribute in the dead of night in order to weaken the Islamic faith and convert Muslims. In a trailer belonging to the defendants, were found hidden illegal Bibles. The court returned a guilty verdict and the yacht and trailer belonging to the British national has been confiscated, along with his motor scooter. The group was also fined $40,000 and given a two month suspended prison sentence.

An e-mail from a Jordanian diplomat friend informed me of an article published in Amman on the front page of a national newspaper, again quoting from 'official Moroccan government sources'. The wording was identical to the version coming from the Moroccan Embassy in Washington, quoted above. These were direct quotes from my *Procès Verbal*.

Now at last I realized why the enquiries made by Moroccan friends, who I thought would be able to help my case from within Morocco, had not resulted in any action. They were being presented with one of two versions of a false story – either of many tons of books being imported, or of my attempt to overthrow the government. No wonder they were powerless to help. But how strange, I again mused, that no one was questioning my freedom! How could anyone guilty of such a serious crime not be in prison?

Some Moroccan Embassies in Europe were still using the first press release by the authorities, quoting the avoidance of sixty-four Dollars duty on books: a minor customs breach. Such an incredible sentence for a minor indiscretion was believed by no one and derided in the British press. Most believed that this must be a case of religious persecution and therefore it was seen as a major breach of international law. That the case had been judged on evidence not produced in court was also well publicized. Government officials took this up on my behalf at the highest level, both in the States and in Britain.

Several more British Members of Parliament became interested and raised the case officially with the Foreign Office. Some also wrote directly to the King of Morocco and the Minister of Justice. As far as I am aware, no response was ever received from any of the Moroccan officials. Lord Alton, an eminent professor, wrote at length to the Minister of Justice. To my knowledge, he also did not get any response. It became more apparent that the only way to fight was by protesting through the press. I hoped the intervention of government officials would give me some sort of protection if I were arrested for this.

Abdullah phoned to inform me that at last the appeal date had been set for July 1st. I asked to meet him in order to find out exactly what he proposed to present in court. He agreed to see me in Tetouan, where I subsequently met with him on 23rd June. We sat together in his car while I took notes of our conversation. I later wrote in my diary:

> Met with the lawyer, Abdullah, outside the appeal court. He was reluctant to give more information other than to inform me of the issues he would be raising at the appeal.

These were written out in Arabic and he translated them for me while I made notes.

1. Violation in court of Article 115. This is an argument over the declaration I am required to make when entering a port. I claim to have made the correct legal declaration, (guns, ammunition, drugs and spirits) whereas the customs say everything contained in a vessel should be declared.

2. Violation of Article 240: the judge's arguments were incorrect, in his opinion.

3. By UNESCO (Florence) Agreement, signed by Morocco, there is no duty on books of an educational, scientific or cultural nature. Bibles are considered educational books in a non-Christian country. Apparently this has been argued successfully before, in the courts, in relation to other religious books.

4. No search warrant was obtained for Jacques' apartment, so the books found there were inadmissible as evidence in court.

5. Due to the violation of our rights under the law – denying us access to a lawyer, a translator or our embassies during the interrogation – the *Procès Verbal* is invalid. The first court already accepted this.

6. The valuation of the books was grossly incorrect, valued at sixty-four Dollars. Since they were of no commercial value and there was no duty liable, this figure should be zero.

7. The case against us is one of a 'minor customs violation', yet there were no customs officers in court to give evidence. There was also no statement of evidence presented by the customs department: only the police report, which was rejected before the court hearing by the King's Prosecutor.

8. The *Procès Verbal* was not read to us and we had no translation of it, and no way of knowing its contents. Furthermore, my copy was unsigned.

9. Several lines in the official court documents had been erased and changed, including names of officials present and the lawyer's name.

10. I am being charged, not with what I carried on the yacht, but with what was contained in another person's apartment, and in his camper van, despite the fact that the apartment holder admits that he already had books there before my arrival in Morocco.

11. The court found that we had imported books that are illegal in Morocco, whereas there seems to be no evidence that Bibles are illegal in the country.

'Any one of these points will get the case dismissed,' Abdullah assured me.

He also pointed out that the appeal could not go ahead without the other defendants being present, or summoned to appear in court: a process which could take months. He asked if I could obtain a statement from Jacques regarding his purchase and importation of the other books found in his apartment and in his camper van, particularly the Study Bibles referred to in the police report. He thought this could have a significant bearing at the appeal.

Shortly afterwards I was able to obtain a signed declaration from Jacques, complete with invoices from Ceuta for the Study Bibles, verified by lawyers and with a diplomatic seal from France.

On Wednesday 24th June, I again visited the British Embassy and met with a senior embassy official and the Vice Consul. The conversation began with a complaint.

'There are reports in the British press that you are not satisfied with the help we are giving.'

'Yes, it's true,' I responded 'I have been amazed at the lack of support from you.'

I reminded them of the statement by the Vice Consul on a previous visit that 'you acted illegally and got what you deserved.'

'What do you expect us to do?' the Vice Consul intervened.

'Even if your statement is true,' I said, 'I would expect assistance in protesting to the authorities about the treatment we received.'

'You have turned this into a religious issue,' she scowled.

'No,' I replied, 'the Moroccan "official statements" to the press have done that.'

She scoffed at this, saying that press reports should be ignored. 'We cannot interfere in any court case: justice here is fair.'

'I am not asking you to interfere or intervene in the case, but to ensure justice,' I told the officials. 'Nothing has been done to assist me whatsoever. As a British subject, I would expect some initiative in the form of a protest based on these points, which I gave the Vice Consul when we last met.'

I handed the Consul a page that I had prepared. This stated:

1. The fine and other penalties totalling nearly half a million Dollars are totally out of proportion for a minor offence involving sixty-four Dollars.

2. Our treatment by the police was a violation of rights under the law, i.e. compilation of a police report without an interpreter and being forced to sign it without a translation and under duress: being falsely told it was a release paper. Held without food and water.

3. 'Moroccan Official sources' were reporting the case as a religious one, whilst the embassy and the lawyer were denying any religious element was reason to question the 'authorities' who were distributing these reports.

I also told the Consul that I was distressed at the many conflicting stories about my case, to the point where it had become impossible for me to believe anyone.

I then asked the official if he would consider sealing my yacht as British property, in accordance with a diplomatic procedure which I had been told about. This would prevent the Moroccan authorities from selling it prior to the final appeal. He had never heard of such a procedure but assured me he would enquire. Would he be prepared to assist me in negotiating with the customs authorities, as advised by the Canadian Consul, who had told me this was one way to come to an agreement over the penalties imposed? Both requests were later refused. My friends at the American and Canadian diplomatic missions were amazed at the lack of interest or action on my behalf by the British Embassy.

It seemed to me that the diplomat accepted the points I made, but that the Vice Consul clearly did not. She launched into her scripted speech, stating that what happened to me was quite 'fair'. She then insisted that I should not take up embassy time with this case, but go in future to the Consular Official in Tanger, who would inform her of anything relevant.

The Vice Consul further told me that the British Embassy, as well as the Moroccan government, were clearly annoyed by the publicity overseas, and blamed me for it. I protested that this had been generated by the magnitude of the penalty imposed for a minor customs offence, and the false police report that was quoted in the

Moroccan newspapers. I emphasized that I was given no option other than to encourage the publicity as a means of my defence.

She repeated once again as I was leaving: 'You got what you deserved!'

Some days after my meeting at the embassy, I received a phone call from a Stephen Jakobi, representing Fair Trials Abroad, an organization based in Britain. He was in Rabat for a meeting at the Ministry of Justice, to pursue another case in the country. Would I like to meet with him? I agreed to go to Rabat and set off almost immediately.

As I was driving, the British Vice Consul phoned. She informed me about the impending visit of Mr Jakobi, and advised me against seeing him: she had heard that I was planning to do so. She said he was here in order to secure a lighter sentence for two British drug dealers, and that I should not allow my case relating to Bibles to be confused with one that related to criminal activity and drug dealing.

She also said, 'I cannot imagine what purpose would be achieved by meeting him, except to give him greater publicity.'

What should I do? I was already on the road to Rabat to meet him. Realizing that I could not afford to completely alienate my British diplomatic representation, I decided to abandon the meeting and return to the marina.

I phoned Stephen on the number he had given me, to tell him my change of plan. He was clearly upset by the embassy intervention and annoyed that I felt obliged to cancel the trip to see him. He saw the Justice Ministry officials the following day, and later told me that he nevertheless presented a paper regarding my case to the officials there.

I thought it ironic that the embassy did not want my case involving Bibles to be mixed with drugs cases, when the Vice Consul insisted that Bibles were as illegal as drugs. Judging by the actions of the police, the court and the penalties, Bibles were far *more* illegal than drugs!

18. Absolute Proof

Thursday 25th June

Several friends and colleagues visited me from overseas to offer help and advice, including a diplomat from the United States. Others came from Lebanon and Britain to give their support. I was hoping that my Lebanese friends could read the Arabic court documents, but they had great difficulty understanding and translating the text. They did find some more interesting revelations from my 'confessions' though; mostly relating to the way things were phrased in order to obtain a conviction by the court.

Things were hotting up in the United States, and one American colleague was able to make a direct link with the US Senate and to arrange for more letters to be sent to the King of Morocco. Whether they ever reached him, we never knew, but I did find out later that correspondence had reached the King's Chief of Staff.

One evening a call came from Adil, the translator in Tanger, to inform me that he had obtained the court judgement papers, and that the translation was ready. He insisted that I collect it on the following day, as he was not prepared to run the gauntlet of the police in the marina again. I was excited, realizing that at last I would have the opportunity to see how the *Procès Verbal* had been utilized by the court. I needed the proof that it was the instrument used to obtain the conviction, illegally. What good that knowledge would do me, I had no idea, but I set out for Tanger early the following day to collect it.

Returning to the yacht I began to study the English translation of the court judgement. The first two pages detailed our names and the accusation of bringing into Morocco a quantity of 'religious books'. Several articles in the penal code were mentioned as having being violated: 65, 67, 251, 252, 254 and 280, but without stating what these were.

Under a heading: 'The Facts', it stated that I entered Marina Smir and 'dropped anchor' with Matti and Veikko, after which the yacht had been closely watched. It continued by saying that the police observed my motor-scooter being used by Matti on one occasion to ride to the nearby apartment of Jacques. Matti was apprehended and Jacques' apartment was subsequently searched with the discovery of a quantity of books, including sixteen copies of 'medium-sized ones, entitled "Holy Book".'

The statement continued, 'Since the defendants did not have mastery of the Arabic language, a translator took the oath for that purpose.' Then came the crux of the statement: 'Having ascertained the identities of the suspects, which were the same as those in the *Procès Verbal*, *the court charged them with the same accusations contained therein and which they were facing*' (emphasis added).

This meant that the charges were indeed those listed in the *Procès Verbal*.

The document then referred to the defence's claim that there was no case to answer. The lawyer had stated in court that the police statement was inadmissible, since we were not given a translation of it, and also that the search of Jacques' apartment was illegal, as no search warrant was obtained. No mention was made of the fact that my *Procès Verbal* was unsigned.

Under another heading entitled 'The Court', the document then noted the declaration of the judge:

> The court decides to reject the plea of the lawyer, on the basis that the purpose of providing the accused with copies of the *Procès Verbal* is to enable them to be acquainted with the contents thereof, and since all the suspects have signed the said statement, with all the declarations therein, and did not contest them, then such signatures amount to them receiving copies of the said statement and agreeing to their contents.

The document ended:

> For these reasons the court has rendered the following judgement: to condemn the accused for possessing and importing goods without a detailed customs permit, condemns each one of them to two months imprisonment and, in addition, a collective fine of [illegible amount] or a one year term of imprisonment in the event of non-payment. The court finds Françoise Delors not guilty by reason of not having any knowledge of the offences.

I now had absolute proof from the judgement that far from being irrelevant to the court, the *Procès Verbal*, although in Arabic, 'unread', unsigned and full of accusations against myself, was in fact the only evidence produced in court. The conviction was based entirely on the fact that I was supposed to have read it and confirmed its contents as being correct. Had that been the case, the conviction would have been reasonable, if not the penalties. There was not even a representative from the customs authorities in court to give evidence against me.

Why, I wondered, were the Vice Consul and my lawyer so sure this document had not been used in court as an aid to conviction? Was this one of the 'verbal' charges spoken of by the Canadian Consul?

Now I also saw the duplicity in the judgement. The only possible offence mentioned in the final judgement was that of importing goods without having filled out a detailed declaration form for the customs authorities. This was a very minor offence indeed, worthy of the ten-Dollar fine spoken of originally by the King's Prosecutor. Nevertheless, all the additional 'crimes' we were supposed to have confessed to were also accepted by the court.

Was the document written in this way in order to be deliberately and cleverly deceptive? It could actually be taken to mean anything: from signing a confession admitting heinous crimes against the Kingdom of Morocco (which would warrant the heavy penalty we received), to the former minor offence.

That evening a call came from 'Prime Time America'. I had never heard of this programme, but was told that one hundred million people tune in each day. The reporter requested a live interview at peak USA viewing time: late at night in Morocco. By now I was used to interviews, having given several to the BBC and CNN. I again went to my favourite place on the beach near the Ceuta border at the appointed time to await the call.

I was able to discuss with the interviewer the different aspects of the case with far more knowledge. I felt that I finally knew what I was up against and could explain the situation exactly: a minor indiscretion on my part, but a major deception by the judicial authorities.

The interviewer first asked if I realized that the Moroccan Embassy in Washington had been inundated with faxes from all over America asking about my case, and protesting the penalties imposed for importing a few Bibles. I had no idea. It was a relief to hear that so many people were taking up the cause, since it had become evident that I could not get justice in the court, and had a lot to lose.

I explained to the listeners that the real problem was the acceptance in court of an unsigned police statement in Arabic, which we were told was a release paper, but which was in fact a confession implicating me with terrible crimes against Morocco. Since everything was in Arabic, my friends and I had no idea at the time what was going on, either in the police station or in the court. Otherwise, we would obviously have vigorously contested the claims. I now knew that our silence, in ignorance of the contents, along with the signatures on some of the confessions, was taken as sufficient grounds for a conviction. I explained that it had taken me many weeks following the trial to discover these facts, and that I now also knew that according to Moroccan law, I could not contest the allegations. Telling the story to the presenter and expressing my thoughts and feelings brought into focus just what a grim picture it was.

I sank into a depression for several days after receiving the translation of the judgement. At times I could not help feeling that the deception wrought against me was so great that it would be impossible to overcome, especially knowing that the appeal court had no power to review the evidence presented.

To add to the gloom, several local people told me there had never been a case that had resulted in the over-turning of a judgement at appeal. I had reached the lowest point since the beginning of all these troubles and had hit rock bottom.

19. Advocacy from Abroad

Friday 26th June

An American diplomat friend, Bob, who I had known for some years, came to visit and to offer advocacy. He had contacts in diplomatic circles and wanted to visit colleagues at the American Embassy in Rabat. I appreciated his calm, professional manner. It was good having someone to talk to who was not involved with the case. His embassy could not directly assist me, since I was a British citizen, but they clearly wanted to help, as he discovered. This resulted in some interesting meetings with a specialist at the embassy. He had been able to obtain information on the case, which supported everything discovered by the Canadian Consul.

He could not comprehend why my Consul insisted that the British Embassy could not get involved, as he believed there was a very clear violation of the process of law in this case. He went on to tell us much more about the power of an embassy to protect its citizens in cases like this, including sealing property with a diplomatic seal pending the full outcome of a legal process. This, he said, would prevent the customs authorities from disposing of the yacht before the full legal process was completed.

Using his advice, I tried once more to persuade my embassy, through the Vice Consul, to make use of a seal to protect my property, but she still refused, claiming in annoyance that the court process was perfectly in order, and denying that there had been any violations of due process or of my rights.

An American consular representative was able, unofficially, to advise me how to overcome some of the obstacles I had been facing when trying to enlist the assistance of friends in Morocco. It was a great relief to find another diplomat who was sympathetic and seemed to know what was going on. He saw no reason for the case, believing it to be 'contrived' and said that my embassy should press for it to be dropped. It had the power to make such a request. I could not help laughing at this suggestion, imagining myself making this demand of the officials, who were already so hostile towards me.

The official told me that there was a good liaison between the judicial authorities and the embassies and that the American Embassy, at least, always knew what was going on, and regularly discussed cases involving their citizens with the authorities.

Two days before the appeal Hassan phoned to suggest that I should visit the regional governor and make my plea to him. I spoke with others about this idea and most agreed with the proposal, but suggested that it would only be worthwhile if I carried a large brown envelope with me. I was not prepared to do this. That same day the British Vice Consul phoned to inform me that she would be attending the appeal hearing. I was pleased, though surprised that at last she was showing an interest. Or had she been told to attend? I found it difficult, in view of her hostility towards me, to believe she would come voluntarily.

On the evening of 30th June, prior to the first appeal hearing, the British Consular official arrived in Tetouan, and we met for dinner. She was much friendlier than when we had met at the embassy, although no less critical of the fact that my friend had brought some Bibles into the country, which she still considered illegal. Most of our rather stilted conversation revolved around the religious implications – or lack of them, as she believed – of the case.

The Vice Consul again raised the matter of a well-publicized port operation in Spain, often shown on Spanish TV, where gifts, including New Testaments, are offered to travellers awaiting the ferries between Spain and Morocco. I argued that this was carried out in Spain and that there were many groups giving out free literature, bottled water, advertising literature etc. It had nothing to do with my case. She disagreed, but did not elaborate.

I offered to show her the translation of the court judgement, which proved beyond doubt that the *Procès Verbal* had been used as evidence against me. She was not interested at all in seeing it, but continued to insist that it had no relevance and was not used in the trial. I gave up attempting to convince her.

Wednesday 1st July 1998 was the day of the first appeal hearing. We did not really know what to expect. The lawyer would ask for the appeal to be heard immediately, but warned me that the normal procedure would be for the judge to ask where the co-accused were and issue warrants for their attendance in court. I set off for Tetouan, together with Anne and Ghada, who had come over for the hearing.

When we arrived the court was packed. A trial was in session involving seven defendants implicated in a drugs case. They all claimed to be hitch-hikers – innocent parties – who took a lift in a vehicle belonging to a drug dealer. It was interesting to observe the proceedings. The judges, two men and a woman, were much older than those at our trial. According to our lawyer, judges are not chosen from among the legal profession, as in most countries, but are appointed from amongst the ordinary folk in the local community.

The procedure during the case in progress was for the judges to ask questions of the defendants, before asking the lawyers to speak on their behalf. After patiently listening to the defence, the central judge dismissed the defendants, who filed out of the court through a side door near the bench.

I was feeling very dehydrated and quite faint while we waited in the heat. At last we were called forward. Nothing was said to me, just the exchange of a few hushed words between the lawyer and the judge before we were dismissed. The lawyer informed us that as expected, the case had been adjourned until July 15th, so that time could be allowed for an order to be issued informing the other parties of the appeal. A brief exchange took place between Abdullah and the Vice Consul before she slipped away without saying anything to me. Any slight hope that the case would be summarily dismissed rapidly dissipated.

I was totally exhausted after this short hearing, and again felt a strange deadened blackness surround me. Having studied psychology, I was acutely aware of what was going on, and was familiar with the signs. A strange merging of sounds caused a deafness a numbing of all my sensations, which produced the feeling of being wrapped in cotton wool. I had felt this before in dreams, and then woken up to a feeling of being trapped inside myself.

I remembered Hiria, a close Spanish friend who had told me of her feelings of 'blackness', during her years of deep clinical depression when she was going through a mental breakdown. I had met her during the latter part of her illness, and now knew for the first time something of what she had experienced. It seemed strange for me to be observing as if from outside, what was going on within, but I could not help feeling so thankful that I was at least in some control of my mind when I knew others were not so fortunate.

Anne, noticing my difficulty in speaking, tried to persuade me to return to Spain with her. I immediately rejected her plea. But when I thought about it, I knew that I desperately needed to escape from the pressures building up around me. After a few Spanish friends who had come over for the appeal had promised to mount a concerted press campaign if I was not allowed to return, I finally agreed. Once I had made the decision, I tried to fill my mind with thoughts of home, in order to offset the worries flooding in about the risks involved, and the onset of what I knew to be a seriously disturbed mental state.

As we journeyed back to the yacht, I had to consider leaving her unattended for the first time. I knew the risks, but did not know whom I could leave on board. I wondered whether to inform the police, who were sympathetic, but decided to inform only one of the guardians, if I could find my 'fat friend' at the end of the jetty when we returned to the marina. First though, we stopped off at the hotel to collect the rest of the yacht gear and paid the bill.

Arriving at the yacht, I collected my eldest daughter Ruth, who had been with me for several days and made sure that everything was switched off, before locking up. This would be my first trip out of Morocco for a month, and was fraught with uncertainty and fear. I decided to leave the car in the port, so that it was not too obvious that I was away. One friend watched for a taxi, which soon drew up alongside the car. We transferred the bags from one car to another, while I looked around, expecting one of the police to witness this event and come running over. To my surprise and relief, none did, although I am sure they missed nothing.

My fears grew as we drove towards the border. Would I be arrested on charges of failing to pay the fine or for trying to avoid the prison sentence? Would the police stamp my passport with '*Persona non grata*' – meaning no further access to the country? Would the customs authorities in the marina discover I was out of the country, and grasp the opportunity to seize the yacht?

Arriving at the frontier passport control, the officer at the computer could not find my entry information. Usually, as soon as the passport details are typed in, the screen fills with information on that person. The immigration officer can then see when he had entered the country and if he had entered with a vehicle. The officer kept looking at the entry stamp, and re-typing my name but eventually gave up looking, and stamped my exit beside the entry anyway. I breathed a sigh of relief, hoping that I would be able to return again.

As we crossed the border, an unexpected, overpowering sensation suddenly besieged me. I had difficulty fighting back the tears and remaining in control of my emotions. I could feel my face contorting involuntarily. Again I was well aware that I was close to a breakdown, and at all costs had to resist the feelings threatening to overwhelm me, at least until I was home. As we walked across no-man's-land, reaching the Spanish border police, another emotion enveloped me: a feeling of exhilaration and freedom. It was like stepping from a hot dimly lit room filled with cigarette smoke, into a garden full of light and fresh airy fragrances. I continued to fight back the tears, as we continued walking to the nearby taxi rank. The friendliness of the Spanish border police was such a contrast. There were no queues here, just an imperative to hurry people through with the minimum of hassle: the very antithesis of Morocco.

Many more emotions flooded my mind and body during the half-hour ferry trip to Algeciras. I tried desperately to remain in control by concentrating on all the things I would do in the garden as soon as I arrived home. Our son Mark was at the ferry terminal to meet us, and drove us the short journey home.

At first I could not speak of Morocco at all: a country I used to love so dearly. I spent hours in the garden looking at the greenery, breathing in the sights and smells, and just wandering around. I felt numb and almost unable to function. It was not long though before I got down to work in my office, forcing myself mentally back to the present needs and away from the events that had been totally dominating my mind for weeks.

It was necessary to send faxes to the lawyer in Britain who had offered to come for the appeal on 15th July, sponsored by Christian Solidarity Worldwide (CSW). As well as offering me an international lawyer, CSW had also done a lot to inform the press and government ministers in England about the case and the lapses of due process. Another friend, the private secretary to a Member of Parliament, was also working to inform the European Parliament. I also had to follow this up with faxes to consolidate the facts of the trial and judgement, of which I was now much better informed since receiving the translated transcripts.

I knew almost nothing about CSW, but was happy that someone, somewhere, had requested their involvement.

It transpired that the organization specializes in highlighting cases where action is taken against Christians or churches, in a way that is perceived as religious persecution. British government officials were among its supporters, and Baroness Cox was its President. I was grateful for their provision of a respected international lawyer who would be assisting, with Abdullah's blessing.

I did not feel that this was principally a case of religious persecution, although I was increasingly persuaded of this view because of the British Vice Consul's attitude and anger that Bibles were involved. In most Islamic countries, Muslims are not allowed to change religion. Although I was not directly accused of proselytising, it was implied in my 'confession'. The fact that the books were Bibles and were stated in the court judgement to be 'illegal in Morocco' was clearly presented by the Moroccan press as a religious issue. I was portrayed as one trying to subvert the nation by undermining Islam and, by implication, the authority of the King. Because of this, I felt that CSW was the right organization to be involved.

I spoke on the phone for the first time with Ramez, the international lawyer. A native Arabic speaker, he was also acquainted with Islamic court proceedings being an expert also in *Sharia* law. I knew absolutely nothing about him, but felt very confident that his involvement would be a great help to my case and busied myself sending the Arabic court documents to his office.

Being home for the first time since the trial was itself like a release from prison. Morocco had been my four walls. Although being constantly reminded of my plight, I nevertheless felt able to distance myself from the troubles, at home in Spain. After two days I was becoming anxious at being away from the yacht and wanted to return.

20. The Dream

Saturday 27th June

During the weekend, a phone call came that triggered a chain of events that were to change my perspective on everything. Our villa in Spain was a large rambling place on three levels. For convenience, there were phones connected at each level and I happened to pick up a ringing phone in the lower bedroom, rather than in my office. I needed some paper to write down a number and was annoyed that none was to hand. I began looking in a cupboard behind the bed, where I found an old dusty notepad. Quickly looking through it for somewhere to write, I tore out a page that was blank on one side, with hand-written notes on the other. I scribbled down the telephone number, folded the paper, and put it in a pocket.

The following day I needed to phone the number. Searching through my pockets, I found the crumpled page. Unfolding it, I idly looked at the scrawl on the reverse side and noticed a heading: 'Court case: arrested with four others for doing nothing illegal.' Thinking at the time that this was a note I had made about our case, I casually dialled the number on the reverse side, and waited while the phone rang at the other end. As I was listening to the ringing tone, I began to wonder about those words. When could I have made such a note at home, as I had not been here since the trial? Turning the page over again, I noticed something I had missed. It was the heading: 'Dream, 6th October 1990.'

I now began, with great difficulty, to read through more of the scrawl. It noted the time of writing as being half past five in the morning. I was stunned, and forgetting my phone call, replaced the receiver. I began to wonder what I had been doing in 1990.

The dream occurred some months after I had left Cyprus, after living there for ten years with my family. I was now on my yacht in Tunisia, beginning the research for the ports of North Africa for my book. I had decided to spend the winter there. While living in Cyprus I had a dramatic recurrence of a debilitating illness, *Myalgic Encephalomyelitis*,[1] which caused weakness and some-times total paralysis. It also resulted in very vivid and lucid dreams that I often wrote down.

During the slow months of convalescence, I decided to use the time of physical weakness to complete a psychology degree I had begun many years earlier. This brought me into an awareness of Carl Jung's books on dream analysis, which fascinated me. I was impressed by Jung's assertion that we neglect our dreams at our peril. Although I almost never understood any of my dreams, I realized their importance, and for years wrote them down, always keeping a notebook by the side of the bed for that purpose. It took discipline to actually reach for a pen immediately on waking, but this is the only way I could remember them. I usually had no recollection of their contents until reading through my notes.

This particular dream began, 'I was summoned to court on very minor charges with three other men. No

---

[1] Known as Chronic Fatigue Syndrome or ME.

sentence was expected as I was not involved in any misdemeanour.'

It continued to describe the road to the court, and what I was wearing at the trial when charged with 'unknown crimes', along with the others. It described me as being conscious of wearing inappropriate clothes in court – having on a sailing sweatshirt and deck shoes – exactly what I wore for the trial.

Towards the end of the dream was a description of my walk to the courthouse, down a hill. I was sweeping the road as I walked, and then helped a cripple to reach the court. This latter statement was equally extraordinary because it was the very expression used over a year after the case by a Moroccan national, who told me: 'You swept the way to the court for us, where we could do nothing to help ourselves.'[2]

I was so affected by what I had written eight years before the trial that I could not move from the chair for several minutes. I knew this discovery was no coincidence. I had never in all the years of writing down my dreams (a practice long since discontinued) looked back at them. They filled several notebooks and were stored away in a cupboard, as I could not bring myself to throw them away. Using that particular sheet of paper torn from one of these books, in order to write down a phone number, was indeed extraordinary: nothing less than a miracle.

The discovery and significance of the dream was powerful. I now had absolutely no doubt that this incident was not just a freak happening but something that had been predicted. I concluded that the whole

---

[2] This was spoken by one who had been imprisoned for being in possession of a Bible, sufficient evidence for the court that he was a Christian.

adventure had a divine purpose. Elated, I went looking for Anne, to explain what had just happened. Then I phoned friends to tell them of the discovery. Some sounded sceptical, but they had no idea of the circumstances. From that time onward I never looked back, or had a single doubt that God was right there with me in this saga.

Since childhood I had never doubted the existence of God. The lady who was director of the children's home had a faith which I admired, and which she instilled in all the children in her care. I discovered later, when my father remarried and I went to live with him, that he also had a strong faith in God. Despite rejecting this in my teenage years, I found that it was impossible to dismiss God from my life.

There were times when however far I strayed, I would be starkly reminded that he was still there and interested in me. One memorable occasion came on a cold winter day, when I was out on my motor-cycle. I often charged around the countryside at high speed, in the days when there were no speed limits on most roads. I approached a bend near Newbury Race Course at eighty miles per hour, and suddenly remembered that just beyond the bend, the road narrowed as it went over a bricked hump-backed bridge. Although I thought I could clear the curve, it was impossible to negotiate the bridge at that speed without taking to the air. Far too late to brake, I was already leaning over into the bend.

I remember feeling paralysed and taking my hands off the handle-bars as I seemed to float through the air. I saw my life, like a slow-running film, being played before my eyes. Suddenly and inexplicably, I was standing by the side of my bike, parked past the bridge. There was no way that I could have stopped in such a short distance: I knew instinctively that it was 'divine intervention' and could not help but thank God who had saved me. A short time later, a close friend was killed on his motor-cycle at the same spot, when he failed to clear the bend.

It was not for another few years, after joining the Royal Navy, that I made a conscious decision to follow the Christian faith. This happened after someone gave me a Bible and suggested where I should begin reading. I was amazed at how the pages of Scripture came alive for the first time, despite many attempts previously to discover its meaning.

The dream brought back the reality of God being with me: a reality so easily lost in the fog of confusion and stress.

21. Interesting Observations

Sunday 28th June

By Sunday I was anxious to return to the yacht and decided to go back the following morning. It was difficult to convince Anne that I must return so soon, but I knew that I needed to go. My friend Hiria along with her daughter and sister offered to accompany me to Morocco. Another friend, Di, also volunteered to come over and was prepared to stay on the yacht while I visited Tanger and Rabat.

I was delighted to have company, although it was difficult not to feel alone. I knew they could not share in my fears. Would I be allowed to return to the country?

Arriving at the ferry terminal in Ceuta we were met by a friend, who drove us to the frontier. Soon we were out of Ceuta, across the border, and standing in the queue for passport control on the Moroccan side. I decided not to pay to have my passport stamped, as I often did to hasten the formality. There really was no hurry this time. There were few people waiting, which was unusual as it was, one of the peak times for tourists. We waited anxiously as the officer collected the four passports and, as always, disappeared behind a curtain where I knew the computer was located. It usually took several minutes for the checks to be made. To my delight, all four were stamped, and we were once again ready to enter Morocco.

I could not shake off the feeling of oppression that descended on me as we walked across the border towards the taxi stand. There was no need for it I told myself, as I was reminded of the dream. But this was different from the depression I had felt before. This was something from the outside pressing in, not something welling up from within.

We drove into the marina and, as usual, police were everywhere. I was greeted by one officer, who asked in a friendly manner where I had been. I replied that I needed to escape from the prison, and had been on a wonderful holiday nearby. I did not tell anyone there that I had left the country on this or any subsequent visits to Spain. The yacht appeared undisturbed over the weekend, and the guardian, who came over to greet me, affirmed that no one had visited.

We had a wonderful meal together in the marina before I drove Hiria's sister back to the border at midnight, making the decision on the way to return to Spain myself the following weekend. The others remained on the yacht for the night. I realized that in spite of the company I always had with me, I needed to move from this physical location, for the sake of my own sanity.

That week was the beginning of yet another roller-coaster. I received a call from an official in the Ministry of Justice, telling me that King Hassan II had intervened in my case, and that I would be allowed to return to Spain with my yacht on the following day.

Some hours later, when I downloaded my e-mail, a similar message was conveyed from a Senator's office in the United States. A fax had been received from the Moroccan Embassy in Washington, congratulating the

Senator on a positive outcome in my case following his letter to the King. I was ecstatic. For the first time I had something in writing! My original intention of a five-day visit had by now dragged on for over five weeks. Was I now reaching the end of the saga? I printed the letter and went off excitedly to show it to Mohammed.

'Yes, I know: something is about to happen. We are about to lose you, my friend, and your yacht!'

He congratulated me, shaking my hand warmly.

I began making plans for my departure, whilst awaiting some official notification. I expected it to come directly to the port authorities, and so frequently visited the offices to ask if there was any news. Several days passed and nothing had come. The feeling of let-down, humiliation and depression returned as time passed. All attempts to follow up on the matter ran into a wall of denial and silence from the officials I contacted. Even the Senator, who I spoke to by phone, could not get a response from the Moroccan Embassy when he tried to follow up on the letter he had received.

Still buoyed by the knowledge of my dream, I decided to return home again to Spain for the weekend, as previously planned. Anne wanted to go back to our home in England, as she had done every summer after school finished. During the past eighteen years of living abroad she had always returned with the children, when the heat became unbearable for her. Temperatures were by now over one hundred Fahrenheit most days, with very high humidity.

Crossing the short distance to the Ceuta border, I once again felt an incredible sense of relief. Although Morocco was feeling less like a prison now that I knew I could come and go, the oppression I felt was still very tangible. The weekend sped past, and I was soon on my way back to Morocco, somewhat refreshed.

Returning again to the marina, I was surprised to find a large motor launch alongside my yacht. It was one usually moored next to the gun-boat on the far side of the marina. I had often observed military personnel washing it down. Several men were on board, wearing matching t-shirts. I was unsure if they were military, police, or customs officers.

A van arrived at the dockside, and the boat was loaded with bales of *hashish* covered in plastic from the rear of the van. The launch then sped off, returning some hours later. As the vessel arrived back a crowd of uniformed customs officers met on the quayside, and I could see a share-out of cash taking place. I photographed the scene from a discreet vantage point on the yacht, anxious not to be seen.

The event was repeated the following day. This time I was able to take more photographs of the whole sequence of events through the clear plastic panel on the spray-hood of my yacht. After this delivery, wherever it was, the launch returned to its usual place, next to the military vessel on the far side of the marina. Perhaps it was an innocent disposal of the drug, but I estimated the boat could easily have reached Gibraltar or Spain during its absence. It was more likely, I thought, that it would have discharged its cargo to another boat for onward transit. This was how I knew many boats operated from the marina. It was ironic to compare my plight over a few Bibles with these happenings taking place right alongside my yacht.

I remembered the words of our chief interrogator as he showed me the marijuana being loaded below the window of the interrogation centre, 'This is worth money, whereas your Bibles are worth nothing – nothing!'

I phoned my lawyer to ask if he had heard anything regarding my release.

'Yes,' he affirmed, 'I received a call from an American Senator's office, a friend of yours, informing me that they have been told you are free to depart. The order, they say, comes from our King! But I have to tell you that all my attempts at verifying this with the authorities have come to nothing.'

Once again I was reminded of the increasing difficulty I was experiencing coping with the wild leaps from hope to despair. I tried hard not to allow myself the luxury of believing anything positive I heard, but this was almost impossible. I needed hope. I busied myself writing copious notes in the form of a diary, and corresponding with friends around the world, along with making transcripts of my conversations with officials. By now I had hundreds of pages of correspondence by fax, letters, e-mails and newspaper cuttings in English and Arabic, as well as all my notes of every conversation since the beginning of the incident. For what purpose, I did not know, but there was little else to do while I waited from day to day.

Although I was free to travel, I was reluctant to leave the yacht any longer than necessary, fearing that it could be boarded and removed by the customs authorities. To overcome the boredom, and to allay the fear and paranoia I often felt as a result of being surrounded by so many police officers, I developed a few games. One of these involved fitting names to faces. I determined to learn the name of every officer and guardian in the port. There were about fifty of them. None would ever tell me his identity, but by listening to them shouting to each other, usually in greeting, it was easy to build up the information. I took photographs of each one, using a telephoto lens.

This knowledge brought about some unexpected results. When passing any of the officers, most of whom wore civilian clothes, I would greet them, always using their names. Most were indignant and asked how I had discovered their identity. Some would deliberately walk away out of sight when they saw me coming. On one occasion, an officer came running over waving his gun and demanded the camera, which I refused to hand over. I quickly turned my back on him and retreated to the safety of the yacht.

Taunting the officers may have been a potentially dangerous game to play, but it was primarily to overcome my own fears, and to help me maintain a sense of balance rather than to be intimidated. It was never intended to cause any offence or embarrassment to them. By the time I left the marina, I knew the names of all the people there and felt some were genuine friends.

My experiences in the marina taught me not to be so hard on foreigners who worked in other Arab countries that are police states. I had known many Americans and Europeans who took up jobs abroad, often for adventure and change, as well as for higher incomes. After a few months most became convinced that they were being watched, or that many of the people around them were actually police officers. This seemingly irrational fear affected their ability to integrate with the nationals. I had always felt some degree of derision towards them, believing they had succumbed to paranoia, and felt unable to accept their perceptions. But if my experience was anything to go by, they were in all probability correct.

It was helpful to discover more about the division between the police and customs authorities. Two policemen in particular became very friendly towards me, and talked freely of their disgust of the customs officers, whom they said were corrupt. One day, while sitting in the café with one of them, I discussed the drug trafficking that I had witnessed going on in the port. He did not dispute it, and told me that some ports were very profitable places to work.

I asked why a few Bibles had led me into such problems, and was told that someone wanted my yacht. The books were a minor issue. This was the second time I had heard this and was intrigued. Some days afterwards I returned from a shopping trip to find a man standing beside the yacht, having his photograph taken. As I approached he quickly returned to a large new Mercedes nearby.

I thought little of it at the time, but was informed later that day by the restaurant owner who saw the event, 'That was the man who wants your yacht!' He would not tell me who he was.

My daughter Ruth, who had written to the Foreign Office to obtain information regarding specific details of my case, phoned me early one morning a few days before the appeal. The Foreign Office had informed her that information had been forthcoming from Moroccan officials about my case. It confirmed that the only charge against me was for a minor customs offence: that of not filling out the correct customs declaration on arrival. They could not explain the magnitude of the sentence, but noted that there was an appeal pending. The letter also confirmed that the *Procès Verbal* had been rejected by the court as inaccurate, and noted that it had been taken under duress. The charge of illegal entry had also been rejected following investigations. This was promising news indeed.

I decided to take Hassan's advice and visit the local governor. Having found out where his office was located in Tetouan, I learned that he did not speak English. I would need an interpreter. I decided to ask Adil to come over and translate for me. Although it would be expensive, I knew that he had contacts in the local press and thought it might be a good idea to put my case to him in the hope that he would ensure my side of the story was published.

I met with Adil outside the Court of Appeal and we left for the governor's office a short distance away. On arrival, the governor's secretary informed us that he was away on business, but that we were welcome to return later in the day. While waiting, Adil suggested we drive up to the top of a nearby mountain for tea. As we sat up there in the cooler air, looking down onto the town, Adil talked of the harassment he had experienced when he came to visit the boat with the translation of the police report. He still seemed shaken by the degree of surveillance on him.

Returning to the governor's office we were informed that he had now returned. Before being allowed to see him, I had to explain to his assistant our reasons for wanting an interview with him. His assistant was an unsmiling, sour-looking man, who would not tell me his name. We were ushered into a room to await our turn with the governor. The room was hot and without air-conditioning, as we sat sweating on cheap plastic-covered sofas.

After an hour we were taken in, ahead of all the others waiting. The governor was a large, jovial and intelligent man. I told him that I was a friend of Hassan's. It took some time for him to identify who Hassan was, but finally it clicked. He asked the nature of my request and I explained the details surrounding the *Procès Verbal*, which was being used against me.

He smiled as he responded: 'Morocco is a very democratic country in which the justice system is independent of the State.'

Fearing that this was the end of the conversation, I continued, 'But I have been convicted on false statements and evidence.'

'I know your case,' he said, 'and I cannot interfere with the justice system. But you have an appeal taking place on Wednesday, no?'

'Yes,' I nodded.

He smiled broadly and told me, 'If you lose the yacht, you will have gained a friend. If you regain your yacht, then you will have a friend!'

He grabbed my hand to shake it, indicating the interview was over.

I have often pondered the significance of this remark. Perhaps it was a proverb; there is an Arabic proverb for every situation. It gave me confidence to know that he already knew of my situation, although this was puzzling. Why would he be so interested in the case? On reflection, I doubted if he would have been prepared to see me if he were not aware that a resolution had already been agreed upon.

I decided to drive over to Tanger to take Adil home, using the opportunity to visit my lawyer. As I drove with Adil talking, I began to realize that I was unable to formulate words in response. I concentrated hard in order to give answers but even an acknowledgement was impossible. Occasionally words in Arabic came out, but nothing more. He looked at me strangely but without knowing what was wrong. I kept on driving, whilst at the same time trying to ascertain if any of my other faculties were impaired, wondering if it was safe to continue.

By the time we arrived in Tanger, I was able to construct simple sentences, but still could not pronounce some words properly. I could hear that my speech was slurred, as if affected by alcohol. I knew this was another symptom of ME that I had not experienced for many years. I had learned to live with these recurring and often embarrassing symptoms over the past twenty-five years. I decided to return to the yacht without visiting Abdullah, fearing a return of the symptoms. The following day, I woke up to a phone call from Anne, and was delighted to hear myself speaking quite normally again.

The appeal was drawing near and I wanted to know if there was anything more I could do. I phoned the Canadian Consul. As before, she told me that she could not give any advice officially as I was British, but said apologetically that she was well aware of the difficulties with the British Embassy.

'As a friend,' she said 'my advice is that you should write your own statement: a "statutory declaration", since the court only has the false one prepared by the police. You should be aware, too, that although the *Procès Verbal* had been officially rejected by the tribunal, it was an important document in the trial, and will be at the appeal.'

'Did you follow my advice and visit the customs authorities in Rabat?' she asked.

'I have already asked twice, following your previous advice, but the embassy will not get involved.'

'You must press them further,' she said. 'I am afraid that on appeal, your sentence may be increased. You do not need to go through with this: everything can be resolved immediately by negotiating directly with the customs authorities in Rabat.' She repeated, 'But you cannot go alone. You have to go with an official from your embassy.'

'Please,' I pleaded, 'would you assist me? My consul refuses to help.'

'I am sorry. I simply cannot be involved. You have to persuade your own Consul.'

This was depressing. I knew I would get no help from that quarter.

22. The Court of Appeal

Monday 13th July

With only two days to go before 15th July, I followed the Canadian Consul's advice, and prepared a statement to counter the *Procès Verbal*. It outlined in simple terms that I had visited Morocco many times. It mentioned that the Ministry of Tourism was well aware of my work, which was to promote yachting tourism in the country. It also stated that contrary to the police report, I had entered the country legally, and had filled out a customs declaration on arrival, of which I had a copy.

I then went to Tanger for the statement to be translated and typed into Arabic. While this was in progress I visited friends in the town, later delivering the completed document to Abdullah. He thought it was an excellent idea, and placed it in a file for submission to the court. I was surprised that he had not advised this himself, but knew it was pointless to discuss it with him. I had not quite decided if his apparent unhelpfulness was simply a reflection of a cynical attitude towards all foreigners or not. I realized that I was a particularly difficult client for him to deal with, since I was always looking for answers to questions that he could not or did not want to answer.

The lawyer remained confident that at the appeal, the case would be dismissed, and kept telling me to relax and not to be at all concerned about the outcome. He insisted that by nightfall on 16th July (the day after the appeal), I would be sailing out of the marina. So far he had been wrong about everything, so I had given up expecting anything other than to hear this. It was cultural: most Arabs, in order not to offend, will tell you what they think you want to hear, rather than the reality of the situation. I had little doubt that he did know the reality, but did not want to tell me. I had great hopes that Ramez, the international lawyer, would be able to get to the truth, and that he would explain it to me.

Before leaving I made an appointment to see Abdullah the following day, as Ramez would need briefing. It had been agreed that he would come as an observer in support of Abdullah. I mentioned to him that the British Consul from Rabat would also be present in court. Anne phoned to say that she would come over to be with me for the appeal, before returning to England with Ghada. She would transport Ramez, who would be arriving from England via Gibraltar airport, and another Spanish friend, José Luis.

Tuesday 14th July had developed into a hot and windy day, as I waited for two hours on the Moroccan side of the border for Anne, Ghada, José Luis and Ramez to arrive. At one point I aimed my camera in the general direction of the crossing, framing the shot that I intended to take of Anne and the others, as they emerged through the gate. Surprisingly, the police became very angry about this, sending a tout to tell me to come over to them, a demand which I ignored.

Finally, Anne emerged with Ghada. It took some time for Ramez and José Luis to follow. Both looked hot and harassed. I dropped Anne and Ghada off at the yacht, while the others came with me to Tanger to meet Abdullah for the briefing. Time was short. Once again I drove the two-hour journey over the Rif Mountains to Tanger. I was well used to the road, but this journey never got easier, especially in summer when the roads were always busy.

Ramez immediately took to Abdullah, and the two chatted away in Arabic for over an hour about the technical and legal details of the case. José Luis and I remained quiet for a while and then, speaking softly, I updated him on all my discoveries regarding the *Procès Verbal*. He told me of a lawyer in Barcelona who had offered to help and who had guaranteed that he would get me out of Morocco together with the yacht, if I paid him five thousand Dollars.

At this stage, I still had hopes that the appeal would overturn the case, but this was an intriguing alternative. I told him that one acquaintance in Spain had contacted my wife to tell her that he too would try to get the yacht out of the marina for five thousand Dollars. He knew the customs and police officers in the port, as he had contacts in the drugs business. Both were options to consider, but only if it became obvious that there was no other way. I knew I would never be able to return if I took either of these routes.

I was very relieved that Abdullah and Ramez got on so well, having expected some tension between the two lawyers. On the journey home Ramez explained all that was discussed.

'I am impressed with your lawyer's grasp of the case,' he began. 'I know he will not discuss anything with you, but like many lawyers, he only likes to talk with other lawyers about the cases.'

As we drove, Ramez talked us through the many violations of the Moroccan legal process that had taken place during the trial.

'You should not be worrying at all: there will be no problem in overturning the verdict tomorrow. I am certain of that! No appeal court in the world could uphold the findings of the court, in the knowledge of so many violations of the process of law.'

Returning to the marina, I dropped Ramez and José Luis off at a local hotel for the night. We had a meal together before returning to the yacht, where Anne showed me her huge collection of newspaper articles reporting the case in Spain and England. I spent much of the evening reading through these, and was surprised to see my photograph making the front page of several national newspapers in England, with lengthy articles on the case. I had no idea that it was being reported so prominently. I did not like the way some of the articles made me out to be a Bible smuggler, and the Moroccans to be less than human, but could do nothing about it.

My local paper in Portsmouth had managed to get hold of a very old photograph of me, and was running a 'Daily Diary from Morocco' updating the situation from reports I had been sending to my children. It was comforting to know that so many people were aware of my situation and were being so supportive.

Wednesday 15th dawned, following a long restless night. It was six weeks since I had arrived in Morocco, and we were now approaching the very hot and humid conditions of mid-summer. To add to the discomfort, I was anxious, as I rehearsed in my mind what I would say to the judge, given the opportunity to do so. Abdullah had indicated that this chance was always given at appeal hearings.

We picked up José Luis and Ramez from the nearby hotel at quarter to eight and made our way to Tetouan. At the court we met up with the interpreter, this time a different one since Abdullah would no longer work with

Adil, following the leaks of information to the local press, which he believed were prejudicial to my case.

I spotted the British Vice Consul, who greeted us very formally. She was surprised at the number of friends who had come over from Spain in my support, and almost immediately got involved in an argument with one of them, a bookshop manager from Ceuta. The dispute was over the legality of Bibles in Morocco. She continued to insist that Bibles were illegal in Morocco. I told her again that all attempts to find any law to prohibit them proved it was ridiculous to maintain they were illegal: they were not. I found the Vice Consul's personality so difficult that I was unwilling to discuss anything further with her.

Once again we went for tea with Abdullah, while waiting for the court to convene. Returning from the café to the court we passed a kiosk selling papers and books, where Abdullah stopped to purchase a newspaper. Looking at the magazines on sale, I was surprised to see some that would be considered pornographic, even in Europe. I raised this with Abdullah.

He said, 'Of course, this is a free country. Would you like one? I can buy it for you.'

I then asked him if he thought it was ironic that we were appearing in court for bringing in Bibles, which were said to be 'illegal in Morocco', when pornography was openly on sale – and therefore presumably legal. He shrugged his shoulders but gave no answer.

The court was already packed when we entered at half past eight. Although ours was to be the first case heard, two others took place before we were called. The first was that of a Nigerian woman, who was in the country illegally. The second case involved a young man who seemed to be insane, claiming to be many different people, and demanding to know which one was being charged. He had the courtroom in fits of laughter as his different personalities and voices shouted and taunted the judge. Even the bench seemed amused by the circus. We later heard that he was a schizophrenic who made frequent appearances in court, bringing entertainment to the onlookers.

Finally, my name was called. I immediately asked through Abdullah, for an interpreter. Much to our surprise, this was flatly rejected. The judge told the interpreter to memorize everything, and later to relate to me what went on. She was only allowed to translate questions addressed directly to me.

Did I understand the charges brought against me?

'No Sir, I do not,' I told him.

He then elaborated that it was for bringing illegal books into the country.

'In that case Sir, I am innocent of the charge and still do not understand, as these books are not illegal here.'

He then turned with a nod to Abdullah, who began presenting his case for me.

After only a few sentences, the judge asked him to finish. He pointed to a heap of folders to his left; there were many cases to be heard that morning. Abdullah continued to read on through his paper and again he was stopped. He ignored the judge, and pressed on in a louder tone. Several more times he was interrupted and told to finish. Abdullah looked flushed and angry as he wiped his forehead; but he complied and stood aside.

The judge then turned to me and asked through the interpreter: 'Why did you not make a legal declaration on entry to Morocco?'

I replied that I had made the legal declaration and had a copy: I was required to declare arms, ammunition, drugs and spirits: 'I had none of these things.'

He looked at Abdullah, who began reading again from his paper, presenting more points of legal argument. The judge then began shouting at him, quoting sections from the *Procès Verbal* that lay open on the bench in front of him.[1] Abdullah interrupted and there was a heated exchange as he insisted loudly that the document could not be used as evidence since it was not signed.

Suddenly the proceedings came to an abrupt end. The judge closed the file in front of him with a loud slap and placed it on top of the heap. Realizing that the opportunity to speak was slipping away, I pre-empted the end of the hearing, asking for an opportunity to speak on my own behalf. The judge looked exasperated and I could see that he was about to refuse, so I did not wait for a response; I told him why I had come to Morocco. I held up a copy of the transcript of my book, which I had brought with me. I could prove that my reason for being in the country was not to overthrow the government, or to engage in any subversive activity as stated in the *Procès Verbal*, but to complete research on a pilot book for yachtsmen.

Before I could say more, the judge raised his hand and stopped me. Picking up and slamming down the file containing the court papers, he announced sharply that my statement was irrelevant. When I tried to continue he told me to be quiet: the hearing was over and he would listen no more. Abdullah quickly came over, grabbed my arm and hustled me out with Anne close behind. Ramez, José Luis and the interpreter followed. It was another amazing farce supported by a great cast of actors!

Abdullah was outraged and humiliated as we met outside the court, declaring that he had never before been treated like this. His only explanation was to assume that

---

[1] As found out later from the interpreter and Ramez.

higher authorities had already resolved the case, and that the hearing was a mere formality. He discussed it with Ramez, and both concluded that by the way proceedings were conducted, only one thing could be indicated: we were soon to be told that the case had been dismissed. This seemed to be supported by the messages I had received about the King's intervention, some weeks before.

We were informed that the judgement would be given in two hours and were asked to wait. The lawyers, so sure the case had been won, suggested we go to the first court to retrieve the thousand Dollar bail money. This should have been an easy procedure. We had the paper and judgement from the original trial, stating that this should, be returned to me. After visiting the appropriate office however, the functionary in charge refused to refund it. Abdullah became embroiled in a heated argument, but further discussion was useless. All attempts to recover the money on subsequent occasions also failed.

We passed the British Consular official on the way out. She was most indignant, saying that the court had not given her any respect as the British Crown Representative. She said normally she would have been given a seat at the front, whereas she was squashed at the back of the court.

'They did not even acknowledge my presence.'

I suggested that the court officials might not know who she was.

'What? Of course they know who I am!' Her indignation matched that of Abdullah. She too expressed surprise at the way the judge handled the case.

The Vice Consul departed while we went to a local café, and sat in the shade. Although it was only half past ten, it was already a sweltering airless day. While we waited, my friend Juan from Algeciras passed by, with a group that he had brought over for the hearing. We spent some time together, explaining recent events before he took his group to see something of the town, while awaiting the verdict.

I could not help feeling gloomy and somewhat numb, in spite of the optimism of both the lawyers. Attempts by José Luis and Ramez to encourage me to perk up were unsuccessful. Although deep down I agreed that logically there *should* be a favourable outcome, I still feared the devastating consequences of a contrary verdict, and felt that it was safer to have absolutely no expectations. We returned to the court to await the verdict.

The two lawyers were chatty and buoyant as we arrived. So sure that all would go well, they virtually bounced up the stairs to the upper levels of the court, to find out if the verdict had been pronounced. A few minutes later they descended in a more sombre mood. Ramez was the first to break the news.

'I'm sorry my friend,' he said.

I looked for signs that he was joking, as he looked so glum, but he went on, 'Things have become worse. The sentences have been upheld, and the *Procès Verbal* has been accepted.'

My mind immediately flipped to the words of the Canadian Consul. Once again, she had been absolutely correct.

This added a completely new dimension to the original judgement, which made no mention of the *Procès Verbal* – at least officially. Abdullah raved that the court had acted illegally, since the document was inadmissible, as stated at the original hearing. Furthermore, he insisted, the court of appeal was not allowed to introduce this document, when it had already been rejected at the trial. My whole body and mind froze. I could not speak. I saw José Luis looking at me for signs of a reaction. I had already armed myself mentally, closing my mind once again to the world around me. But nothing could prepare me for this.

We drifted slowly back to the car without further discussion. Ramez had to return immediately to the ferry terminal in Tanger, in order to catch his plane that left Gibraltar for London that afternoon. It was a very sombre occasion. I felt weary and ill, yet somehow relieved that another gruelling chapter was closed. As Ramez departed, he promised to bring this latest injustice to the ears of members of the British Parliament, where he had good contacts.

I decided to leave for Spain, for a brief period, together with Anne and José Luis. I felt defeated and desperately in need of a break. One priority was to get as much gear off the yacht as possible. I had begun this some weeks ago, but suspended the operation following the renewed hope of being able to sail the yacht out of the country. Now, once again, these hopes had faded.

We returned to the yacht, which Di had been taking care of while we were in Tetouan. I told her what had happened, explaining my need to leave for Spain. I decided to try to load the Zodiac dinghy into the boot of the car and take it with us. When a police officer noticed what we were doing, I explained that I was taking it to Spain, although I was concerned that he might feel obliged to consult with his superior. Fortunately, he said nothing and walked off.

I later learned that his reaction was another manifestation of the hostility between the customs officers and the police. The police really were prepared to help me – and did so on other occasions – when I wanted to get expensive items off the yacht and back home to Spain.

We left hastily. Crossing the border into Spain, I once again felt the incredible and tangible relief. I was immediately elated and could even forget the boat, at least for a while.

I thought back to an interview a few days before with the presenter of 'Prime Time America'. Several wealthy Americans had phoned in and offered to provide another yacht if I eventually lost mine through the proceedings. But my yacht was unique. She was a perfect live-aboard and very spacious. Furthermore, she had been home for many years. I was not sure I would take up offers of another.

As I contemplated this I recalled my dream, and wondered if it had contained any indications that I would eventually be free, together with my yacht. Pulling out the scrap of paper, I scrutinized every word. There were no hints about the yacht, not even a coded hope, only the forewarning of the case itself.

I recalled how, when I was in my twenties, I had received a very unusual letter from a friend. I was away in the Far East and it contained information that he could not possibly have known about, prophesying several future happenings in my life. I made the mistake of determining *how* these events would happen and became very upset when they did not occur. Years later, when I re-read the letter, I realized that everything written had been fulfilled, but not in the way I had anticipated. It made me very cautions about the way I interpreted anything now.

The only glimmer of hope that the yacht would be returned came in an interesting note from a Christian friend, who wrote to me a few days after the original verdict. It contained a verse from the Old Testament of the Bible, which read: 'The Lord made him prosperous again and gave him twice as much as he had before. ... The Lord blessed the latter part of Job's life more than the first.'[2] My friend clearly believed this was inspirational, and meant that the yacht would be returned to me. Could I put my hope in this verse?

Before the ferry pulled into Algeciras Harbour, I phoned an American friend and lawyer, to inform her of the outcome of the appeal. She was amazed to hear from me, saying she had been trying to call me all morning. Of course, my mobile had been turned off for the court hearing.

'My Senator was told that the King of Morocco has ordered your immediate release, together with your boat,' she said. Could it be true this time.

I felt another boost of optimism, even though I had heard it before from a different Senator's office.

I felt sure there would eventually be a breakthrough and decided to press on for this to be fulfilled, whatever the personal cost. Nothing would be gained by just giving in to what I now perceived to be a corrupt judicial system. I resolved to keep fighting, whatever the news. I knew we must be reaching a critical time and that the customs authorities would be doing everything possible to collect their prize. I was amazed that I had been able to survive so far.

---

[2] Job 42:10; 12.

23. Waiting for News

Thursday 16th July

Once home, I no longer felt as anxious to return to Morocco as I had done on previous occasions. I was emotionally and physically exhausted. I knew that this was what the Moroccan authorities wanted: for me to give up the struggle. It was becoming increasingly difficult to sustain any level of optimism.

I tried to prepare myself for life without the yacht. This was difficult, as sailing, or at least living on a yacht, had been a major part of my life for thirty years. I knew what was at stake if I did not return to Morocco – for certain, loss of the yacht. I could not give up hope, not only for myself, but also for those who might find themselves in a similar situation.

It was with this feeling of confusion that I left Spain for Morocco the following Monday. What reception would I receive at the border post? Would the police have been informed by now about the latest verdict? Would they refuse to allow me to return?

I spoke with Hassan on the phone as I crossed, updating him on the latest events. He said that he already knew, and asked whether I knew that an official wanted my yacht.

'Yes' I replied, 'other people have told me the same thing, but I have no proof, and in any case I can do nothing about it.'

He suggested that I should change lawyers, as it was obvious that the one I was using was 'very weak'.

'No judge would have dared to speak to a respected lawyer in the way that Mr Abdullah was spoken to in Tetouan,' he told me.

Hassan seemed to know a lot, which surprised me, as Tetouan was only a small provincial town. He explained that he had heard on the Moroccan news about the latest verdict, and said it was grossly unfair. He was also now aware that the charges were false. I asked him what he knew about the charges, but he would not say more on the phone.

'I have made enquiries. You are right, there is no duty payable on books. And, contrary to the court judgement, Bibles are not illegal in Morocco.'

Hassan then told me of a well-known and respected human rights lawyer in Rabat, and advised me to visit him, taking the case details and photographs of the yacht with me.

Arriving back in the marina, I was met by Mohammed. He told me that things were not looking good, and asked what I was going to do. I told him I was appealing again, and I still expected action from higher authorities. He told me there would be more pressure from the customs authorities to surrender the yacht if nothing happened soon.

An hour later a motor yacht that I thought looked familiar arrived in the port. I recognized the captain as Andy, a friend from Spain.

'Would you moor next to my boat and take some things back to Spain for me, Andy?' I said.

He immediately agreed. Having a friend close by was a great boost to my morale. He couldn't believe that we had been accused of bringing in a few Bibles, when everyone knows of the incredible amount of contraband that goes into the country, and the tons of drugs coming out. Slowly we transferred my outboard motor, the life raft, and several other larger, more valuable items from my yacht to his. I was careful, however, not to remove anything that would prevent me sailing out. I still remained hopeful.

The following day I phoned the Canadian Consul, again confirming that everything she had told me so far had proved correct. She reiterated that my only hope was to negotiate with the head of customs in Rabat. I told her that the entire contents of the *Procès Verbal* had been accepted at the appeal, and that this had nothing to do with the customs. She agreed and said that there was a lot of confusion.

I phoned the British Embassy and spoke with the Vice Consul to ask again for assistance in dealing with the customs authorities, but this was abruptly refused. The Vice Consul immediately launched into a verbal assault about the many press reports and publicity on both sides of the Atlantic, stating that this would harm my cause. I replied that I had absolutely nothing to lose and everything to gain by this reporting; I was powerless otherwise.

I then questioned the Consul again as to what my embassy had done to assist me. She reiterated that they could not interfere in the case. I was not asking for intervention or interference, but a protest by the embassy to the appropriate Moroccan government authorities, based on the facts I had previously presented to her. She did not respond to this.

Abdullah phoned and asked me to visit his office. I needed to pay him the money to cover the cost of the final appeal in the *'Cour de Cassation'*[1] in Rabat. Once in Tanger, he told me that this was the highest court in the land, overseen by judges with substantial legal backgrounds, unlike the lower courts. He had prepared the legal arguments and was convinced that once the case reached Rabat my troubles would be over. As I was about to return, my mobile phone rang. Di was calling from the yacht to inform me that seven customs officers had boarded, together with Mohammed. They had a paper authorizing them to take control of the yacht following the appeal, and were carrying out a valuation, she said. They needed me to sign the paper. I left immediately and hurried back to the yacht.

By the time I arrived it was four o'clock in the afternoon and the officers had already left the port. The duty customs officer said I was not allowed to board the yacht. Talking with Mohammed, I gathered that the regional head of customs had visited the marina from Tetouan together with other officers. They brought a signed order from the court giving them permission to sell the boat.

'But the final appeal had not yet been heard: they had no right to dispose of the yacht until then!'

Mohammed was very apologetic and asked for a copy of the judgement. This had not been made available even to the lawyer, I told him, so it certainly would not be in my hands. I did, however, have a paper signed by the court to prove that an appeal was in progress.

'This paper is important. Show it to the customs officer, as they should not be able to take the yacht before the legal process has finished.'

---

[1] High court of appeal.

I began to feel very insecure and rushed off to find this paper before events overtook me.

I went with Mohammed to show the paper to the duty customs officer. He would not even look at it.

'Everything is finalized, as far as customs is concerned,' he declared.

I asked if the yacht had been valued.

'Yes, for the amount of two thousand Dirhams,' ($200) he announced. An appointment had been made for me to meet the head of customs in the port, at nine o'clock the following morning to sign a document. I agreed to be there, not telling him that I had no intention of signing anything. I stated that regardless of the order, I was returning to the yacht and spending the night there. I left his office. The officer chased after me shouting: '*Interdit Interdit*!' Forbidden forbidden!

The next morning, I arrived at the customs office at nine and awaited the arrival of the chief. By ten o'clock he had still not arrived. The duty officer phoned Tetouan and was informed that he was on his way. An hour later he phoned again and told me that his boss had already left his office, but was held up in traffic. By noon I was getting anxious and asked what was going on. The officer advised me to return to the yacht. He would inform me as soon as his chief arrived. I stayed in the office defiantly, reading a book.

I dreaded his arrival, thinking that this could be the end of the road, but I certainly was not going to let the authorities take over without a struggle. I feared that if they saw any weakness, the battle would immediately be lost. I was sure that my determination to stay in possession of the boat had been crucial to the position I still held, now almost four months later. As the day wore on, with many phone calls to head office, the officers continued to insist their boss was on his way. Finally, late in the afternoon I was informed that the meeting had been postponed until the following day.

Again I waited the next morning. When he had not arrived by midday, I offered to go to his office to see him, but the officers would not tell me where this was or his name. Was this another farce in the making? I became quite irate as I waited, finally deciding to return to the yacht in the late afternoon. I never did meet this official.

One morning I heard a loud commotion and shouting further along my pontoon. I went up to discover that a Spanish yacht had arrived in the port, apparently some hours earlier. There had been rough weather in the Straits of Gibraltar during the night, and the crew arrived tired, with their yacht battered and covered in salt from the high wind and spray. A customs officer had seen the yacht's equipment drying out on the dock and had called his colleagues and confiscated it, removing it to the customs office. He said that the yacht had imported it, without paying duty, as it was on Moroccan soil.

I told the captain that this was just an excuse: an opportunity for the officers to make some money. 'You need to offer *baksheesh*: either a small amount of cash or a bottle of whisky. Then you will get your gear back.'

Reluctantly the captain took a bottle of whisky over and all the gear was immediately returned. They left an hour later in disgust.

When I heard that my mother had arrived in Spain, along with another friend from the Middle East who had come to visit me, I returned home to meet them. My mother brought with her several more articles from the press, including a report from *The Times* telling of the yacht's inspection by customs officials and its sale for two hundred Dollars. The Moroccan Ambassador in

London had been contacted to verify the facts and had confirmed the report.

Following a weekend break I took my mother and my friend to Tanger. Mum stayed there to explore while my friend and I continued on to Rabat for an appointment with Mohammed Ziane, a prominent human rights lawyer and the owner of a newspaper. Hassan had recommended that I should visit him, saying that he wanted to publish an article on my case in his paper *El Hyatt*. I was interviewed for an hour and provided a photograph of the yacht. The correspondent showed great interest in the case and could not understand how it had reached the court.

We also visited Abdel Aziz Bennani, head of a Moroccan human rights organization, OMDH. He promised to follow up my case with the Minister of Justice. I told him to expect to hear stories about several tons of books being involved – anything between seventeen and twenty. I advised him first to take a look at the photograph and see if he could envisage such a quantity being stacked on board and then taken to an apartment, with a military checkpoint only a few metres from the front door.

It was now mid-September, four months since this had all started. How much longer could I hold out? I wondered.

Hassan called me one evening, to tell me that he had been meeting with one of the highest officials in the land and that they had discussed my case. At first, the official had quoted the Justice Minister, stating that several tons of books were involved. Hassan had urged him to investigate this claim, giving my explanation that it was physically impossible for this to be true. The cartons would have to have been stacked several metres deep on the deck and clearly visible, yet the customs officials found nothing. Nor could the small single-room apartment in which we were supposed to have stored them possibly have contained so many books. The official had investigated and discovered the story to be false, he confirmed.

'The only offence the customs authorities demonstrated – though, even then not in court – was failure to complete a special declaration to cover the books your friend Matti was taking to his French friend. There was even an argument over whether this constituted an offence. All you have to pay is 100 Dirhams.'

We seemed to have come full circle, for this was exactly what the King's Prosecutor had said in the first place many months ago! I was both elated and furious.

Hassan was one of the top businessmen in the country, as well as a member of the Moroccan Parliament; his friend had a high position at the palace. I found it impossible to believe that they did not know exactly what they were talking about. For the first time in months, I allowed my hopes to rise. But it was premature: the ordeal was not over yet.

24. The King's Intervention

Around 18th September

After hearing the news from Hassan, I went to Mohammed in the port and told him that I was about to be released. He smiled and said that he had heard this before and asked where the papers were to officially inform him of it.

'They will come,' I stated with more confidence than before.

Three days later there were still no official papers. Calls to American diplomats had verified the information, but I still had nothing in writing to authorize my release.

Again I became frustrated and depressed and decided to return to Spain for the weekend. Until now I had not informed my lawyer that I was regularly going home to Spain at weekends. I feared that if he informed the authorities, I might be prevented from returning to Morocco.

This time, however, I felt safe and phoned to inform him that I would be going home for three days. He was delighted, believing it was my first time out of the country since the arrest. I reasoned that if the King had demanded my release with the yacht, then nothing would prevent it. If he had not, then hopes were fading that I would ever be sailing out of the country. It was fortunate that I had told him because on Sunday 20th September, official news finally came while I was at home in Spain.

I was watering the garden when a call came through from Abdullah, who announced cheerfully that I was now free to depart from Morocco. I asked about my yacht and motor-scooter.

He laughed and said, 'Yes, with everything – the King has ordered it. You should immediately return, as we have both been summoned for a private meeting with the Minister of Justice … bring your best suit!'

Now I really did feel elated, and immediately began preparations to depart.

This time I would take the ferry directly to Tanger instead of Ceuta, since it was closer to the capital, Rabat. I would arrange to stay overnight with a friend who lived there, departing early in the morning with Abdullah, who would drive us to Rabat for the meeting. It was late Sunday night when I arrived in the port of Tanger; my friend was there waiting to take me to his house. We chatted until the early hours before retiring to our beds for the few remaining hours.

At five o'clock I walked the short distance to meet with Abdullah as arranged. It was still dark and the streets were deserted apart from some street sweepers as I walked down the hill. After waiting a few minutes Abdullah arrived in his Mercedes and we set off through the centre of town to the highway.

I immediately fired questions at him: 'What's happened? Can you fill me in?'

He said that he knew little, except that the Minister of Justice had phoned him on Saturday to say that officials had been looking for me in Marina Smir in order to bring the news, but had failed to find me. 'The minister had wanted to apologize and explain "some things".'

I had to make do with this, as Abdullah, even if he knew more, was unwilling to share it with me.

It took some time to locate the office and to find a parking place. Abdullah then disclosed that we were to meet with Moulay Tayib Sherkawi, Director of the Department of Criminal and Gross Convictions, in the Ministry of Justice. We found our way along corridors to a grand office, where he was waiting for us. He seemed a delightful man: very courteous, polite and well educated.

After lengthy greetings, Mr Sherkawi ordered tea to be brought in. He then asked me to explain what had happened to lead up to my arrest, but told me not to mention or discuss the court proceedings. I had no idea why he said this, as the conduct of the court case was central to my complaint against the Justice Ministry.

'I have been coming to Morocco for many years,' I began, 'and have written a book with the co-operation of your Minister of Tourism.'

I had brought the completed manuscript along to show him and held it up, but he was not interested in looking at it.

'In May I came with two friends and one of them was found with some Bibles in his possession, for which we were all arrested.'

I told him of the false charges of illegal entry to Morocco and the false admissions contained in the *Procès Verbal* which was not translated and which I did not sign.

'These were then published in the Moroccan press as "confessions".'

I was interrupted and reminded not to mention the courts. I told him that I was particularly distressed that the newspapers in Morocco were reporting from 'official sources' that 'many tons of books had been discovered on the yacht'. In fact none were ever found there and the story was quite absurd. In summary, I said, 'I have been convicted on the basis of what officers found in someone else's apartment and vehicle, which is grossly unjust.'

He leaned back in his huge leather chair and, smiling, said, 'You have done nothing wrong.'

He continued on at length, to explain the place of the Holy Scriptures in the context of Islam. He said the Christian Bible was considered a 'Holy Book' by Muslims and the police and judge were wrong to have stated that the books are illegal in Morocco. He went on to explain in more detail why Christian Scriptures were not illegal.

Amazingly, he was using exactly the same arguments that I had used whilst trying to convince the British Vice Consul in Rabat. She had vigorously contested this reasoning. He went further and stated that the Scriptures – both Muslim and Christian – far from being illegal, are actually protected under the law of Morocco.

Mr Sherkawi said in a very kind and understanding voice that the correct entry procedure was to have made a separate declaration of the books. I should have ignored the usual entry formalities. He admitted, however, that there was no way I would have known this.

'You have done nothing illegal, though what you did was inadvisable,' he said. 'The police were wrong to have arrested you and the appeal court was wrong to have upheld the conviction of the first court.'

I was free to leave Morocco with my property. First though I had to go to the customs office and pay a 'small' sum in order to obtain a clearance document to present to the port authorities. I asked what that amount would be, but got no answer. I asked again.

'Would it be 10 Dirhams or 100 Dirhams?'

'Yes, something like that,' he replied.

After some discussion in quiet tones between Abdullah and the minister, the meeting was suddenly over. He ushered us to the door and we left his office and made our way down a long wide corridor, stepping out into the bright dusty heat of Rabat. Abdullah assured me that we would be able to get the required papers easily, since the customs office was nearby. We first went to a café for tea.

Arriving at the drab customs house we found that the chief was not present, so we talked with his deputy. He knew nothing about the case, but said that we should go to the authorities in Tanger, since the file for Tetouan Province was held there. Then we should make an offer for the release of the yacht that would then be considered by the head of customs in Rabat. I was immediately suspicious. Just how many people had been in my position before and why was the procedure so defined, if indeed, he knew nothing about the case?

I was becoming confused again. Why should we be negotiating a price for my release if the King had already authorized it? Abdullah could not explain this and seemed to agree with my logic. I became suspicious that someone, having failed to get the yacht, was now determined to make money out of this situation before allowing me to depart, regardless of the King's orders. Abdullah said patronizingly that we should go to Tanger as the deputy had advised.

I would have preferred to stay in Rabat, in order to see the head of customs there. Abdullah disagreed and said we were doing the right thing. I could not help thinking that he was somewhat afraid of something and did not want to stay in Rabat, but I had no way to convince him, or to know what his fears were.

As we headed out of Rabat one of my diplomat friends phoned from the United States.

'Hi Graham. I have some great news. I have just had the Moroccan Ambassador on the phone again congratulating me and the Senate on a job well done. It seems that the charges against you have been dropped. You are free to leave Morocco, with the yacht and your motorcycle!' Yet again I was hearing these words.

I recounted the meeting that had just taken place, and she was overjoyed.

After thinking over the conversation, I discussed with Abdullah the consequence of paying a ten-Dollar figure, and having all charges dropped. He said that if the charges were dropped, there should be nothing to pay, and that it would be wrong in principle to even pay one Dollar as this would imply acceptance of guilt.

As we continued on our return journey north, I enquired about the defence he had wanted to present at the original trial. Would this have affected the outcome? He said that if we had followed his advice, we would not have been in all this trouble. I explained that because we believed we had done nothing wrong, we did not consider a conviction possible. It seemed absurd to give a false defence, when the truth should have set us free.

'You made your own choice, and this is what happened,' Abdullah commented.

I rather regretted my naivety.

Abdullah agreed to visit the customs office on my behalf, in order to obtain the necessary paperwork for my release. He took me to the yacht, but would not come on board when I invited him. Perhaps he was just anxious to return home. I could not help feeling, though, that there was a deeper significance. Abdullah had told me previously that few lawyers want to take on cases where religious issues are involved. Did he want to keep his association with me as far away from the public eye as possible? Was he afraid of reprisals? I immediately went to the marina office to inform the staff of the visit to Rabat.

Returning to the yacht, I phoned the British Embassy in Rabat and asked to speak with the First Secretary. Once connected, I reported the outcome of the meeting I had just come from. He was delighted and began telling me how hard the embassy had worked on my behalf.

A short time later, the Consul called me back to report that he had sent the Vice Consul to the Justice Ministry, and that she had spoken to Mr Sherkawi.

'Mr Sherkawi denies to the Consul that the conversation had taken place, and stated that everything you reported was incorrect: the charges have not been dropped and Scriptures *were* illegal in Morocco. You are still in deep trouble!' 'But my lawyer was with me and can confirm everything,' I exclaimed.

'I know, I know,' he said irritated. 'I have already called him and he has confirmed your story.'

He had told Abdullah too. Everything we had understood was incorrect: we had both misunderstood. I felt very embarrassed and did not know quite what to say or even to think.

I then phoned Abdullah, who was furious with me.

'Why did you tell the British Embassy of the visit? You should not have done that.'

'I had no idea it was supposed to be a secret meeting,' I told him, 'and it was natural to want to inform my embassy that I was free.'

I asked him why the conversation at the Justice Ministry had since been denied.

'Of course he denied it, what do you expect?'

I didn't know what to expect anymore. Just what was going on?

I never discovered why the substance of this meeting was so vigorously denied. Everything the minister had told us seemed so logical and correct. I wondered if the Vice Consul herself had objected to the conciliatory words of the minister to us. I was not aware that the meeting I attended was supposed to be secret. If I knew that I would not have informed the embassy of what I understood to be the ultimate good news.

I returned to the yacht to await news of Abdullah's visit to customs, expecting a fax to be forwarded to the customs and police office to order my release. It never came.

25. Bargaining with Customs

Tuesday 22nd September

The following day, Tuesday 22nd September, Abdullah phoned to tell me that the customs were now demanding 150,000 Dirhams ($15,000) and would accept nothing less.

'You have to pay it by tomorrow, or the yacht will be taken away,' he said.

This was shocking news and totally unexpected.

'It is impossible for me to obtain that amount of cash in less than a day,' I explained. 'I need more time to enable me to discuss it with friends.'

I needed at least a week, even if I did decide to pay such a large sum of money. He immediately agreed to this. How, I wondered, was he able to make decisions on behalf of the customs? I tried to get hold of Hassan and others, to find out why there was a sudden demand for money. I suspected it was simply because the orders from the King had not yet been received by the customs authorities. I hoped that given a few days, the information would filter down. Hassan could not contact the officials who might have had the answers, since they were at an important meeting in Paris.

I waited in the marina for two more days before returning to Spain, feeling despondent. Soon after arriving home, Abdullah phoned me to insist again that I had to sort out a deal with the customs immediately, or I would lose the yacht. I crossed on the ferry to Tanger and met with him. He took me to see the head of customs in Tanger, Moulay Akhzur. After formal greetings, Mr Akhzur turned to me and demanded: 'How much are you willing to pay for your yacht?'

Taken aback, I hesitated for a moment.

'Pay? What for? There should be nothing to pay. I have not committed any offence. The Ministry of Justice has confirmed this. It was your King who ordered the release of my yacht and there was no mention of any payment,' I said.

'I am not interested in that: how much are you willing to pay?'

Feeling exasperated, I again objected to paying anything, but told him I would give one thousand Dollars just to settle the matter and as a good-will gesture. A long conversation ensued in Arabic between Abdullah and the chief.

Finally Abdullah turned to me and said, 'One hundred thousand Dirhams. That is what you have to pay: it is a good price.'

We were ushered out of the room. Obviously there was to be no more discussion.

Once outside the office, Abdullah said I needed to make an immediate decision, or they would take the yacht. I refused. I needed time to think, and to get some advice. He then told me that this amount was only for the yacht.

'No. Any payment must include everything, including the motor-scooter,' I responded.

'OK, it will also include the motor-scooter,' he said. It now seemed that it was he who was setting the figure and orchestrating events.

I had made several phone calls to officials and was awaiting news about the situation. I needed to know if King Hassan II had really intervened. If so, how would this be communicated? Most of the King's staff were still in Paris, so I was unable to find anything out.

I received a call from an embassy official, asking what was happening. Thinking that the official may not know about my previous visit with the lawyer to the Justice Ministry, I informed him about this. He said he knew about this meeting and asked if the conversation was in writing, as it had been denied. What sort of question was that? I did actually have it on a dictaphone, but did not tell him that.

More bad news awaited me. A call from the United States disclosed that their Senator's enquiries were also being met with denials. This was extremely worrying. If I delayed paying the $10,000, I could lose the yacht. If, on the other hand, I paid, I may later discover that I should have paid nothing, embarrassing those who had done so much to ensure my release. It was a serious dilemma. Was this simply a wait for the King's orders to arrive at the right place, or were the customs authorities able to override his directives? Just what was going on?

On the last day of September I returned to Spain, feeling very disheartened. I spent a lot of time watering the garden, which had been scorched in the summer heat, and catching up on mail. As I did so, I decided that it would be better to pay the cash to the customs, even though I knew deep down that I should not pay anything. If I could just hold out, I was sure that the wishes of the King would eventually prevail and I would be released.

By now, however, I was on the edge of collapse and I did not know how much more I could take. I discussed it with several friends, who all agreed that it was best to pay the money. I knew they were thinking more about my welfare than the justice involved, but I was also aware that I could not continue in this dreadful state of emotional turmoil.

I made arrangements for a loan of the required amount to be transferred to my account in Gibraltar, and went there the following day to withdraw the cash. Bob, who came over to liase with the American Embassy several weeks before, had a friend in America who offered to pay whatever it cost to get the yacht out, if that became an option. The loan was therefore only needed temporarily. I phoned Abdullah, asking him to arrange a meeting with customs for the morning after the withdrawal. He told me to make sure the money was in Moroccan Dirhams: 'Banknotes,' he insisted. I asked him if I would get an official receipt, as I did not want to pay only to find out that I was unable to take the yacht out. He laughed, but did not reply. Again my suspicions were aroused about the activities of the customs authorities.

I decided to ask whether the British Consul in Tanger would be prepared to attend the hand-over of the cash, providing official recognition that it was for the release of the yacht.

'Yes of course. That shouldn't be a problem.'

Another call was necessary to confirm that I could legally convert that amount of US Dollars into Dirhams on arrival in Tanger. I was concerned that there may be problems at the border, or with walking into a bank with ten thousand Dollars in cash and asking for it to be changed.

Once again I decided to go directly by ferry to Tanger, arriving on Sunday night. The passage from Algeciras often took over three hours, and it was a rough trip on this occasion, coming up against strong westerly winds. Moroccan immigration police, who were always on board, carried out passport control on the ferry, meaning that we avoided any queues and hassle in the port. I was nervous carrying so much money in through customs control, but there was no problem as I left the ferry and headed for the port gates.

I checked into a local hotel on the seafront. It was a sleepless night on a hard mattress and I was happy to see dawn break.

Early in the morning I met with the Moroccan friend who had arranged to assist me to change the cash into Dirhams at his bank.

At the appointed time, the British Consul came to the hotel with Abdullah, and we departed together to the customs house. I had not seen her since she had visited me in the Tetouan police station four months before. Since then, I had been dealing with the Consul and Vice Consul in Rabat. The Consul seemed very friendly, just wanting to get on with the business. It was a relief to have her assistance. I wondered now if I should have made her my point of contact all along, rather than the embassy.

We met briefly with the head of customs, who again asked how much I was prepared to pay. I said I would pay a thousand Dollars. He again announced that he would not accept less than ten thousand Dollars. Not wishing to delay things, I immediately agreed, knowing that there would in any case be no further negotiation over this figure. He said he would contact the head office in Rabat who would have to approve the sum, and then communicate their acceptance to the Tetouan office, where we would have to pay the money.

'The release document for the yacht will also be issued in Tetouan,' he told us.

I then asked for assurance about the release, to ensure that it included the scooter. He asked about its value, which I put at two thousand Dollars – it was almost new. He expressed surprise. I immediately regretted giving its true value, realizing I should have said two hundred Dollars.

'I will have to contact head office about this as the fax is not working. Please return in an hour for confirmation.'

This further delay worried me, but the Consul seemed unperturbed, which was reassuring.

On our return an hour later, we found that nothing had progressed: the fax was still broken, but the chief assured us that all was in order, and we only needed to go to Tetouan to pay, and to pick up the certificate of release. The Consul spoke with the chief, apparently obtaining the necessary assurance she needed about the yacht and scooter. She seemed happy, so we took her home.

'If you run into any problems I will come over to the marina,' she said.

This at least gave me some assurance that she believed all would go according to plan.

It was half past one before we set off for Tetouan with the cash. Finding the customs house in a back street of Tetouan took some time, and several of the staff, including the director, were still out at lunch when we arrived. We were ushered into a room to await his return. He seemed to be expecting us when he arrived, and took us immediately to another office for the cash to be counted. We were there more than an hour while the cash was counted and the receipt issued. This receipt was a long strip of paper, stating that it was for: 'payment of duty on the yacht'. I was not sure what that meant, but it seemed that I was not paying a fine, but some form of duty. Had I now paid import duty on the yacht, and if so, why? This was another bizarre twist. I never found out the answer to that question.

Following the completion of formalities, Abdullah took me to the marina. He wanted to return home immediately, but fearing problems, I asked him to accompany me to the customs office in order to present the release paper, and ensure the scooter was returned. As I suspected, all was not straightforward. The duty officer objected to releasing the scooter, but said I could take the yacht. Abdullah showed him the receipt, which specifically mentioned the scooter, as well as the yacht. After some argument between them the bike was returned to me. I breathed a huge sigh of relief. Was I finally free?

26. Final Departure

Friday 2nd October

I was walking on air as I said goodbye to Abdullah, and headed to the yacht from the marina offices. Di had arrived earlier that morning from Spain, and I had great news to tell her: we would soon be departing for home!

After meeting Di on the yacht and sharing the news, I returned to the office to find out how much it would cost me to settle the marina bill. I was prepared for a fight. The marina fees were amongst the highest in the area. I intended to argue that the customs authorities should cover my four months here, since they had detained me against my will.

The official bill was nearly three thousand Dollars. The girl running the office was not in a position to negotiate, but tried to phone her boss, who was in Casablanca. Unable to reach him, she suggested that I contact the head office of the company in Marbella, Spain, where the marina financiers were based. I was given the name of the boss there, and called. Immediately, he recognized my yacht's name, and said that he was familiar with my situation. Pleased at the outcome of my situation, he promised to work out a deal. Some hours later, I was delighted to hear that he had agreed to a huge reduction of the bill. I paid the invoice by credit card and prepared to depart.

More complications soon arose. By the time the account was paid and our passports were stamped, it was dusk.

The local Gendarme officer said, 'I'm sorry. It is unsafe to depart as it is dark. There are strong winds too.'

My mind raced as I tried to find a way to depart that night, in case there were more nasty surprises in store. I really did not trust anyone. Was this another trick to try to keep me there? Or was it a genuine reason for detaining me further? The possibility of having something planted on me or the yacht occurred to me again. I concluded that if I had to stay another night, I would be very vigilant indeed.

Darkness and the strong wind had never deterred me from sailing before. The officer pointed out that Moroccan gunboats were on patrol in the area, and had instructions to detain any vessels in the region at night. I knew that this was true and realized that a decision had been made, and that there was absolutely nothing I could do. Finally I agreed to depart at first light the following day – regardless of the wind. This was accepted, and the police said that they would come to the port early in the morning to see us off. I did not believe that for a moment!

I spent part of the night making preparations for sea; jobs that I would otherwise have done once underway. Several ropes had deteriorated over the summer, and I had not replaced them. I remembered the advice of several of my sailing friends, especially following the revelation that a valuation of just two hundred Dollars had been arrived at by customs officials: 'Sabotage the yacht. Sink her! Do anything to prevent some corrupt official from taking her!' they had insisted. It was

Finally free again and sailing home towards Spain after more than four months trapped in Morocco.

tempting to consider this option, but I was pleased not to have heeded the advice.

The first entry in my ship's log for over four months read:

> Friday 2nd October
> 0500 Awoke and made preparations for sea. Collected passports.
> 0600 Passing port control tower, to cheers from police officers.

0630 Underway, course 350 T, heading for Spain.
Wind W 4-5, 15 to 20 k.

It was an amazing and emotional experience as we passed through the marina entrance, close to the offices of the police and customs. There was a crowd of police officers gathered on the end of the jetty. Some in uniform took their hats off and cheered as we passed just a few metres away. Several were off duty; they must have come especially early to witness our departure.

The wind was strong and increasing westerly as we headed out to sea, clearing the huge breakwater and raising the mainsail. Turning towards the Ceuta Peninsula we then headed north towards the Rock of Gibraltar. It was the end of a long nightmare.

Epilogue

Five years have passed since I sailed out of Morocco. During that time I have returned by air and ferry on several occasions to the country and have presented copies of my completed book, *North Africa*, to the Moroccan authorities. Officials at the Tourist Ministry were very happy with the final result and promised to give one of the copies to King Mohammed VI.

I had no intention of writing about this minor indiscretion. It was during a trip for a conference shortly after the events that I started to sort through old files on my laptop. I came across hundreds of notes, letters and e-mails surrounding the case and began to file them. As I did so, I was overcome by an unexpected urge to write about it.

Over the next three days I wrote the text of the book from memory, later comparing it with notes written at the time. To my amazement, every detail was correct. It was a cathartic experience. I then left it for four years, with no intention of publishing anything on the subject.

Soon after my departure from Morocco I discovered through my lawyer that I was still listed as a criminal in the country. Immediately I checked that an appeal had been lodged with the highest court of appeal, the *Cour de*

Cassation in Rabat. I learned that it had been filed, but even now, five years on, my lawyer has been unable to get any date fixed for the appeal, or to discover my status. Until then I cannot sail into Moroccan waters with my own yacht once again, without fear of reprisals.

There are many unanswered questions that I still face. Why did the court ignore the King's Prosecutor and pronounce fines and penalties so high? Why was the unsigned document, the *Procès Verbal*, accepted by the court? How did the charges of illegal entry become accepted fact? Why did the official at the Justice Ministry, who initiated the meeting in Rabat, subsequently deny it? Why was the British Embassy so hostile and unhelpful throughout the case?

I would like to discover why I had to pay the customs authorities 10,000 Dollars. Being compelled to pay under continued threat of immediate confiscation of the yacht, even when the authorities knew of the intervention of King Hassan II, was contrary to expectations.

The precariousness of my situation was highlighted in May 2001 as I was passing in transit through Casablanca airport from Malaga. I was again arrested, taken from the boarding area and interrogated for some time by police. I refused to answer any questions unless I was told why I was being held, which was never divulged. I was released after a while and allowed to continue my journey. Later inquiries indicated that I should not return to the country unless and until my status with the authorities was clarified.

Many letters written on my behalf by the International Court of Law and Justice to the judicial authorities and to the Minister of Foreign Affairs have failed to elicit any response. Letters from British government Members of Parliament to officials in Morocco have gone unanswered, as have my letters to the authorities.

I have allowed this book to be published now, believing that I have little to lose by doing so. Almost nothing is written here that is not already in the public domain. There were reports of the case at the time broadcast and published by the BBC, Prime Time America, CNN, Reuters and Associated Press, as well as in several international papers and the Moroccan press. Articles also appeared on the internet.

I mentioned at the beginning of the book that this minor indiscretion left a deep and life changing impression. Why?

Although the time in police custody was relatively short, the four months I was trapped in Morocco before being allowed to leave with my boat gave me a lot to think about. I discovered that the Bible was one of many books which, although not officially banned in the country, was nevertheless rarely given an import licence. Thankfully things have changed under the leadership of King Mohammed VI. I would like to express my gratitude to King Mohammed VI for his father's intervention in my case, without which the outcome would, I am sure, have been very different.

I never denied having Bibles with me, or that Matti was carrying some to the apartment of a friend in the marina. But the frustration of having false accusations laid against me in order to gain a conviction was something that ate away at my mind for those four months. Yet, as a Christian, this should not have been so troublesome. After all, there are many examples of injustice and persecution in the Scriptures. There are also many people in the world today imprisoned through false accusations. Many will never be released. Having experienced the trauma in small part enables me to sympathize and protest on behalf of those poor souls.

Since the events of 9/11, it has become easy, if not commonplace to imprison anyone who is remotely suspected of any terrorist activity. They are given no rights, no embassy visit, no lawyer to represent them. Many families are not informed of their whereabouts. This happens in North European countries and in America. What does that say to third world countries? Given the false charges made against me, I could have so easily disappeared under similar circumstances today.

But God knew well in advance that this event would happen. It was too much of a coincidence for me to have dreamed of the event so many years before, and to discover my record of it in the given circumstances. That he had spoken to me in this remarkable way was not something new. The Bible is full of examples of God making himself known to his people in trouble, as well as making known the future. It is impossible to exaggerate the comfort and encouragement of knowing beyond any doubt that I was not alone in these circumstances, whatever the outcome.

Having so many friends who were prepared to act on my behalf was something truly wonderful. To know that so many people who I had never even met were protesting was a great privilege. Even today I regularly receive e-mails asking how things are and if I am able to return yet to Morocco. I am very grateful to my friends in the West who spoke up for me and for those inside Morocco who, at considerable risk to themselves, were prepared to push my case right to the top.

I continue to appeal, now through the pages of this book, for assurances that it is safe for me to return to Morocco, a country I love.

Glossary

Aiwa	Arabic for 'yes'.
Amigos	Friends.
Baksheesh	An expected gift such as cigarettes, alcohol or money given for a service.
Cour de Cassation	High court of appeal.
'Bien! Bien!'	'Good! Good!'
Dish dash	A traditional white one-piece robe worn by Gulf Arabs.
Douane	Custom authorities.
'El problema es la aduana'	'The problem is with the custom authorities.'
Hashish	The consumable product derived from the marijuana plant.
Injil	The Arabic name for the New Testament as found in the Qur'an.
Interdit	Forbidden.
Kif	Term for a type of marijuana.
Muktar	Town Mayor.
Naam	'Yes' in Middle Eastern Arabic.
Oui	French for 'yes'.
Persona non grata	Often stamped on passports by the police meaning no further access to the country.
'Parlez-vous Français?'	'Do you speak French?'

Procès Verbal	Police report or statement.
'Que pasa?'	'What is happening?'
Salam Alikhum	'Peace be upon you (all).'
Sharia	The Islamic religious law, based on the Qur'an rather than the secular law.
Shroumer	A long roll containing spiced meat and lettuce.
Souk	Market place.
Surte	Police.
Tawrat/Torah	The Arabic word used in the Qur'an for the Old Testament.
'Wa Lahma Kaman?'	'And meat also?'
'Yallah'	'Let's go'
Zabur	The Arabic word used in the Qur'an for the Psalms.
Zillij	A term used to describe a pattern formed by brightly coloured ceramic tiles.

THE EUROPEAN CENTRE FOR LAW AND JUSTICE

, rue de Rome
57000 Strasbourg
France
Telephone & Fax
33 (3) 88.61.08.82

JOHN WARWICK MONTGOMERY
Ph.D (Chicago), D.Théol. (Strasbourg)
Barrister-at-Law
Senior Counsel

No. 9, 4 Crane Court
Fleet Street, London
EC4A 2EJ, England
✓ Tel. +44(1525)405.443
✓ Fax +44 (1525) 840.338

✓ E-mail: 106612.1066@compuserve.com

TO: Maître Abdullah Bakkali
In re: Graham Hutt

Dear Sir:

Attached is Mr Hutt's full description of his case, with his expression of concern that the case be expeditiously calendared by the Cour de Cassation.

He informs me that you are of the view that the case may simply be "buried"--never to be calendared at all.

Is there no procedure in Moroccan law by which the Cour can be *compelled* to list the case? Surely, something can be done to reverse (or reverse and remand) the matter so that justice can be done?

We of the European Centre for Law and Justice are fully prepared to attend the hearing as observers, or, even better, as co-counsel before the Court, and to do anything else within reason to bring this matter to a successful conclusion. But we are powerless to institute proceedings in Morocco: we can only assist you in your capacity as Mr Hutt's counsel of record.

I am bilingual (French and English), so you may reply in either language. Feel free to use phone, fax, or e-mail--e-mail being the quickest and least costly.

Yours faithfully,

Prof. Dr John Warwick Montgomery   11 October 1999

cc Ben Bull, Director, ECLJ Strasbourg
   Jay Sekulow, Chief Counsel, ACLJ
   Graham Hutt

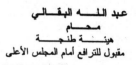

ABDELLAH BAKKALI
AVOCAT
BARREAU DE TANGER
AGREE PRES DE LA COUR SUPREME

عبد اللـــه البقـــالي
محـــــام
هيئـــــة طنجـــة
مقبول للترافع أمام المجلس الأعلى

طنجة في 2 / 11 / 1998

مذكرة ببيان أسباب النقض

<u>جناب السيد الرئيس الاول
لدى المجلس الأعلى
(الــــربــــاط)</u>

<u>لفائدة</u> : السيد كراهام هات ، إنجليزي ، راشد ، طبيب متقاعد
مهنة والجاعل محل المخابرة معه بهذا المكتب.

طالب النقض..عنه ذ/ عبد الله البقالي المحامي بهيئة
~~طنجة~~ والمقبول للترافع امام المجلس الاعلى الموقر.

<u>ضد</u> : إدارة الجمـارك في شخص ممثلها القـانوني بحضـور
المحامي العام للملك لدى المجلس الاعلى.

<u>جناب السيد الرئيس الأول والسادة الرؤساء الغرف لدى المجلس الاعلى الموقر :</u>
<u>يتشرف العارض بأن يبسط أمام جنابكم ما يلي :</u>

1- <u>من حيث الشكل :</u>

حيث ان القرار الاستئنافي صدر بتاريخ 15 / 7 / 1998 .

وحيث ان العارض صرح بالنقض بتاريخ 17 / 7 / 1998 وأدى الوجيبـة القضائيـة
بنفس التاريخ حسب ما هو ثابت من الوصل المرفق طيـه وكذا شهادة بكون الحكم غير جاهز
عملا بمقتضيات الفصل 353 من قانون المسطرة الجنائية والفصل 579 من نفس القانون.

وحيث ان العارض وما دام قد اودع الوجيبة القضائية ومادام ان طلبه موافقا لما يقتضيه
القانون فانه يتعين معه التصريح بقبول نقضه شكلا.

---

11 ، شارع خالد ابن الوليد (فيلاسكيس سابقا) الطابق الاول رقم 2 -طنجة -الهاتف – 78 27 93 – فاكس 81 55 93
11, Rue Khalid Ibn Oualid (ex. Velazquez) 1er étage apt 2 Tanger Tel : 93 27 78
Fax : 93 55 81 Patente 50427775 C.N.S.S 1706667

المملكة المغربية

وزارة العـــدل

محكمة الاستئناف بطوان

قرار جنحي

رقم 3852/98

بتاريخ 15/7/98

قضية رقم 2837/98

حضوري ، غيابي

النيابة العامة

. أصـل قـرار محفـوظ بكتابـة الضبـط

بمحكمة الاستئنـاف بــ (ح ش)

بـاسـم جلالـة الملـك

بتاريـخ ———— عام ألف وتسعمائة ————

موافـق ———— سنة ألف وتسعمائة ————

أصدرت محكمة الاستئناف بتطوان ————

القضية الجنحية التطوانية

جلسـتـها العلنية الحكم التالي :

على نفسـه :

الوكيل العام الملك

والمطالب بالحق المدني ———— من جهة

المطالب بالحق المدني

المتهم

التهمة

الفصل

القـرار

حبسا

غرامة

القرار سجل

بتاريخ

صفحة ——— عدد

مبلغ الواجبات :

دفع بتاريـخ :

وصل عـدد :

نسخة تنفيذية

من القرار ————

في ——— صفحات ————

سلمت ————

للسيد ————

(وقائـع القضيـة)

بناء على الاستئناف الاكلاف المقدم من :

النيابة العامة

والمتهمـــين

(نتائـج القضيـة)

نمـوذج 40079/96

32,5 x 24,5 — 64 غرام

Mod.C. 3.

المملكة المغربية
إدارة الجمارك والضرائب غير المباشرة

**ADMINISTRATION DES DOUANES
ET IMPOTS INDIRECTS**

Bureau de .... *Tétouan*

Numéros :	
de quittance	3 2 0
de déclaration	1949 D
de liquidation	3 2

QUITTANCE DES DROITS ET TAXES : PRODUITS DIVERS

N° 0877485

Reçu de M. *Maitre Abdellah Bakkal P/e Hutt Graham Cyril*

demeurant à .... *Tanger*

la somme de .... *Cent mille quarante Dhs* _____

_____

montant des droits, taxes ou produits divers détaillés ci-contre, dûs à divers ....

Amende + T.S.I

Dont quittance Le *05.10.98*

Le Caissier

Nature des droits	Montant liquidé
RS3	100.000,00
R.6.03	40,00
TOTAL A PAYER :	100.040,00

1,85

35
310

Reçu un et une amende de cent mille
(100.000 dhs)

Monsieur SAANANA

Royaume du Maroc

L'ordonnateur Liquidateur
des Douanes et Impôts Indirects
à Casablanca

le 25/10/99

KR03
623

100.000,00

101
100.000,00

100.000,00